Lee Bailey's
Long Weekends

Lee Bailey's
Long Weekends

RECIPES FOR
GOOD FOOD AND
EASY LIVING

by LEE BAILEY

photographs by LANGDON CLAY

recipe testing and development with LEE KLEIN

CLARKSON POTTER/PUBLISHERS
NEW YORK

Design by
DONNA AGAJANIAN

Published by Clarkson N. Potter, Inc., 201 East 50th Street, New York, New York 10022. Member of the Crown Publishing Group.
Random House, Inc. New York, Toronto, London, Sydney, Auckland
Clarkson N. Potter, Potter and colophon are trademarks of Clarkson N. Potter, Inc.
Manufactured in China
Library of Congress Cataloging-in-Publication Data
Bailey, Lee.
Lee Bailey's long weekends / by Lee Bailey ; photographs by Langdon Clay ; recipe testing and development with Lee Klein.
p. cm.
Includes index.
1. Cookery, American. 2. Menus. 3. Entertaining. I. Title. II. Title: Long Weekends
TX715.B1566 1994
641.5—dc20   93-3193
CIP
ISBN 0-517-59244-4
1 0 9 8 7 6 5 4 3 2 1
First Edition

ACKNOWLEDGMENTS

Special thanks to Bruce Aidells, of Aidells Sausage Company; Pamela Auld, of Chukar Cherries; Ann Criswell, of *The Houston Chronicle*; Mickey Ellis, of *The Huntsville Times*; Mr. and Mrs. Mark Harris, of the Texas Wild Game Cooperative.

In New York, my thanks to: Joe Allen; D. D. Allen; Rina Andussi; Mark DiGiulio, Peter Meltzer, and chef Michael Kalajian of Quatorze Restaurant; Sean Driscoll; Mary Emmerling; Frank Faulkner; Sherwin Goldman, with an assist by Julie; Faith Stewart Gordon; Sibby Lynch; Danny Meyer and chef Michael Romano of the Union Square Cafe; Mardee Haidin Regan; Ted Voss; Bill Walter; Toby Walter; Linda Wells.

In Pass Christian: Mr. and Mrs. Jerry Dattle; Mr. and Mrs. Blair Favrot; Stuart and Jane Maunsell; Kathy Posey and her daughter Jane Howard; Sandra Shellnut.

In Round Top: Eleanor Cummings, Beverly Jacomini, Bud Royer.

In Mendocino: Tony and Karen Bruehl, David Lackey and Kathy Casper, Sandra and Bill MacIver, Linda Prial.

In Rhode Island: Marjorie and Bob Catanzaro, Judy Chace, Kevin Farley, David and Paula Golden, Mrs. Kay Perkins, Tim and Claudia Philbrick, Richard Richardson, Tayo Shore, Paul Wilmot.

In Dorset: Sissy Hicks, Hal and Judy Miller, Gretchen Schmidt.

In Lenox: Byrne Fone and Alain Pioton.

In South Carolina: Robert Barbato, Louise Bennett, Sunny Davis, Libby Demetree, Mr. and Mrs. Pat Ilderton and their son David, Joyce King, Mr. and Mrs. Leonard Krawcheck, Sandra and Tom Player, Fred and Judy Reinhard, Dottie and Mark Tanenbaum, John Martin Taylor.

In Santa Fe: Joan Baker, Sylvia Johnson, Lawrence McGrael, Ann Minty, Roselea Murphy, Barbara Pohlman, Robin West.

In Tesuque: Betty Stewart and Pico and Clare Eddy Thaw.

In Galisteo: Priscilla Hoback and Denise Louise Lynch.

In the San Juan Islands: Patterson Simms, Nani and Bill Warren, Fred and Betty Whitridge, Jim and Binka Nicol.

Thanks, too, to my marvelous coordinator Lee Klein, with an able assist from James Lartin—and from time to time from Terrell Vermont—and my New York coordinator, Helen Skor.

For those always beautiful photographs by Langdon Clay, many thanks.

For my agents old and new, Pam Bernstein and Michael Carlisle.

And finally for my hard-working editor, Roy Finamore, and the wonderful back-up crew at Clarkson Potter who make it all seem so effortless—when I know it's not. My sincere thanks to you all.

CONTENTS

INTRODUCTION

HAVE YOU noticed how vacations have changed over the last decade or so? They seem to be getting longer *and* shorter at the same time. Years ago people took an annual couple of weeks with pay all at once, but this is less and less the norm. Short hops sprinkled throughout the year, maybe finished off with a week or ten-day trip, are becoming more and more popular. And what used to be several hours in a car is now just as likely to be several hours on a plane to visit friends who have houses in out-of-the-way places. I for one am all for the change—four or five days including the weekend sandwiched in the middle can be the perfect amount of time for catching up with old buddies, soaking up a little local color, or getting some color if the sun cooperates—do a little group cooking, read, get in a few sets of tennis or a round of golf, or simply lay about. I suppose this was bound to happen to a generation that has come to think nothing of driving half a day to ski or look at the fall leaves. Or for that matter, of pulling up stakes entirely and moving to another city, state, or coast; and whose retired parents are as apt as not to take off for warmer climates when the air turns chilly or to leave for an unstructured and open-ended jaunt just for the change and fun of it.

One thing hasn't changed though: the ways people seem to like to entertain themselves in vacation houses. Many who thought they had black thumbs now garden, or who never played before take up tennis, or who thought they couldn't relax take to the hammock, or who never particularly enjoyed cooking discover the pleasures of the grill and the stew pot.

As a guest I always bring a couple of recipes with me that I like to add to the mix. So this book is essentially about visiting friends and cooking with them in their vacation retreats—wherever they are— and in the process having the chance to explore a few parts of country that are new to me. In these distant and distinct locations, it's a treat to use produce, and even sometimes recipes, that reflect the region. For instance, in the San Juan Islands, off the Washington State coast, certainly one meal had to be built around the delicious fresh salmon available there, not to mention one of my old weaknesses, blackberries, that seem to grow along every path. And when I spend time in the Northeast I expect to feast on lobster and clams in some form at least once. Such local specialties add a fillip of pleasure and actually can provide a new appreciation of old favorites that holds over when I get back, often even becoming part of my cooking repertoire. As I obviously did, I think you'll find plenty here to tempt you on that score. But of course today we needn't journey to the Pacific Northwest to enjoy salmon or blackberries; luckily all we need is to be reminded of how very good they can be. Especially when prepared in ways that are slightly different from our own tried-and-trues.

Now as long as we're on the subject of house-guesting, maybe here is a good place to pass on a few things I've learned about guests during my years as a weekend host. They're subjective, of course, but here goes. First, come prepared to be a little self-sufficient. If you have wheels, even a bicycle, you can go off on your own and give yourself—and your hosts—a break in the routine. (While you're at it, you can also run a few errands, always appreciated.) If you don't have transportation, bring something along to keep yourself amused and interested without having to depend on the household, such as plenty of reading material, or needlepoint, or crossword puzzles, or fishing gear. Or come prepared with an agenda of your own. For instance, I have a friend who, when he came for a visit, used to first look in the local papers, then I swear would go to inspect every boat and classic car within a radius of fifty miles that was listed for sale, returning in time for a swim and dinner, and as happy as a clam. A perfect guest. I never had to be concerned that he was enjoying himself or try to think of things that might amuse him. Remember, the hosts are there to relax and unwind too, so don't constantly wait around for them to divert you. To my way of thinking, supplying the house and the meals is enough.

About house gifts. There are two ways of dealing with this matter. You can arrive with a small token gift and plan to snoop around to find out what might be welcome and useful to send later. This is especially true of a fairly new house. Or, if you know the hosts' tastes, you might strike out in a more personal direction. For myself, wine and books are always a pleasure to receive. Food, however, which is a popular choice, should be considered from several angles. Remember, over the years homeowners accumulate more than their share of gift food—odd jams, pickles, and the like—so I'd skip this category unless the gift is a specific concoction you know they especially like. On the other hand, you can come prepared to help with a meal or two by cooking a dish you know they enjoy, or even go so far as to prepare one whole meal. If you intend to do this, though, you should clear it with the hosts in advance. This is also true if you are bringing or planning food that must be eaten during your stay. As thoughtful as they may be, such gifts can foul up planned menus or simply be redundant.

And finally, if at all possible try to arrive when say you will (not before). If you arrive unexpected around lunchtime, stop off first for a bite or to take the household out with you for the meal. Usually the hosts have their hands full with last-minute preparations. And at the end of the planned visit, leave when you've said you were going to. As welcome as guests are on Friday, by Sunday night or Monday it's time to hit the road unless you have been invited for an extended stay.

So it's off to the hammock and grill, and a perfect long weekend.

Sullivan's Island,

South Carolina

CHARLESTON SITS SQUARELY ON the plain of central coastal South Carolina in the heart of what is called the lowcountry. Here the land is locked in a fruitless battle against the unforgiving Atlantic. Evidence of this standoff shows in the changing terrain on the drive toward the sea, which takes you through stands of loblolly pine and wild magnolia and down tunnels of bent old live oaks. Soon the soil turns loamy, then muddy, as more and more water enters the picture, seeming to break it apart. Ultimately vistas of flat, green marshes open up, cut through by brackish channels that sometimes make hairpin turns back on themselves; the slightly larger and higher chunks become islands sprouting palmetto palms, more pines, and entwined lower undergrowth.

The marshes around Charleston are fed by rivers such as the Ashley and Cooper with their accompanying streams and tributaries converging to find their release into the ocean. It's a romantic, slightly mysterious landscape that's a nursery to shrimp, crab, and oysters as well as a place of shelter for pelican and heron rookeries, and nesting marsh hens. There are deer, alligator, and they say even a few bear in and around the marshes as well.

The myriad islands that become the coast east of Charleston were once home to determined families who made their living from the sea. Over the years they were joined by Charlestonians who built houses on the islands for respite from the summer's sauna heat. One of the first to become such a retreat was Sullivan's Island. At best, life on such barrier islands has been precarious, for nature likes to toy with them, dissolving and building long stretches of the ocean-front as she does. In the last hundred years or so, the area has been

swept almost clean by hurricanes and lesser winds on numerous occasions. Blithe steadfastness has become second nature.

Those tough souls who make their living from the sea know best how to handle nature's caprices, how to hunker down and endure. And the part-time residents know how to clean up and get on with it. Most older houses on Sullivan's Island are big and breezy and have a wonderfully appealing higgledy-piggledy quality with none of the suburban taint that is so common to planned seaside communities. All have generous screened porches and are massed together as if to present a unified face to the elements. Sullivan's Island is for boating, fishing, beaching, crabbing, cooking, laying about, and roughing it in comparative comfort and ease. There are miles of broad, broad beaches fascinating in that the vegetation gives way slowly, starting with patchy grass, vines, and wild flowers, then rolling into low dunes dotted by beach plum, yucca, and a few low palmettos. After that, the strip of sand is punctuated by salty pools and clumps of low grasses before becoming a wide swath of smooth, fine sand that finally disappears into the surf.

Nearby islands provide a fine variety of fresh produce to go with the great cornucopia of seafood—a heavenly, unhurried place to visit and cook. What follows is a sampling of what we ate there.

Not so incidentally, there's a marvelous cookbook called *Hoppin' John's Lowcountry Cooking*, filled with traditional recipes, lore, and more. I met the author, John Martin Taylor, a Charleston native who got my head spinning and my mouth watering with tales of great feasts he's had as a result of all this abundance from the sea and surrounding land. A few of the recipes here, as noted, are from him.

PRECEDING PAGES: *Lowcountry marshes.* BELOW, FROM LEFT: *Sunset over the sandy banks; rampant blooming beach vegetation; an afternoon on the beach.*

FRIDAY NIGHT DINNER

THAI STUFFED CRABS

GREEN ONION AND CORN FRITTERS

SWEET CUCUMBER AND CARROT SALAD

FRESH COCONUT CAKE

Stuffed crabs have been a staple of menus in the coastal southland for generations, so when Terrell

Vermont, a Southern friend and authority on Thai food, came to visit, I asked her to come up with a

version of the classic stuffed crabs using Thai seasoning. She provided a spicy twist on this old clas-

sic. Accompaniments were little fritters and a sweet crunchy salad. Dessert was an old Charleston

coconut cake made from a recipe that John Taylor revived in his book.

ABOVE: *Typical Sullivan's Island cottage.* OPPOSITE: *The dinner table—with Thai Stuffed Crabs, the fritters, and garnishes.*

Thai Stuffed Crabs

As is the case with many Thai dishes, these crabs are very garlicky. If you are not a garlic lover, cut the amount called for by half.

6 medium garlic cloves, coarsely chopped

6 sprigs of fresh cilantro with leaves, broken into small pieces

1 pound fresh lump crab meat, picked over

1/2 pound boneless pork, very coarsely chopped

1 cup cooked white rice

1 large egg white

3 tablespoons *nuoc nam* (see Note)

Pinch of light brown sugar

1/4 teaspoon black pepper

12 crab shells, washed and dried

Cilantro, for garnish

Dipping Sauce (recipe follows)

Preheat the oven to 375 degrees.

Place garlic and cilantro in a food processor and mince. Transfer to a medium bowl and add the crab, pork, and rice. Mix this lightly but well. Add the egg white and *nuoc nam* and toss lightly. Add brown sugar and pepper and toss again lightly. Place in the shells, mounding them slightly in the middle. Do not press down. Place on a baking sheet and bake for 20 minutes. The tops will not brown.

Garnish with sprigs of cilantro and serve with Dipping Sauce (recipe follows).

Serves 6

Note: Nuoc nam is a fermented fish sauce available in the Oriental food section of many supermarkets or in specialty stores.

Dipping Sauce

1/4 cup sugar

1/2 cup water

1/2 cup red wine vinegar

1 1/2 tablespoons *nuoc nam*

1 teaspoon red pepper flakes

1/2 cup shredded carrots

2 tablespoons shredded radish

1/4 cup chopped unsalted roasted peanuts

Bring the sugar, water, and vinegar to a boil in a nonreactive pan. Stir in the *nuoc nam* and red pepper. Place

carrots, radish, and peanuts in a small bowl and pour hot liquid over. Cool to room temperature before using.

Makes about 1 cup

Green Onion and Corn Fritters

You can make these while the crabs are baking, but not before, as they are best within 10 or 15 minutes of cooking.

1 cup rice flour

1 large egg white, beaten a few strokes with a fork

3/4 cup water

2 teaspoons *nuoc nam*

1 tablespoon minced fresh cilantro, with stalk

Pinch of curry powder

1 teaspoon black pepper

1 1/2 cups fresh corn kernels, cut and scraped from the cob

3 large green onions, coarsely chopped, with some green

Vegetable oil, for frying

Mix the rice flour, egg white, water, and *nuoc nam*. Stir until smooth. Stir in the cilantro, curry powder, and pepper, then fold in the corn and green onions.

Heat about 1/4-inch of vegetable oil in a large skillet over medium heat until hot, but not smoking. Scoop up batter in 1/4-cup measures and add to the oil. Don't crowd the pan. Cook until just turning golden on the bottom, about 1 minute, then turn and cook until golden on the other side. Drain on paper towels.

Makes about 18 fritters

Sweet Cucumber and Carrot Salad

I especially like this combination of flavors with the crabs.

2 medium cucumbers, peeled, seeded, and cut into
  ¹/₃-inch-thick half moons

1 medium carrot, scraped and sliced into ¹/₄-inch-thick
  rounds

¹/₄ medium red onion, coarsely chopped

1 medium pickled jalapeño pepper, seeds removed, minced

1 cup water

¹/₄ cup granulated sugar

¹/₄ cup light brown sugar

¹/₃ cup distilled white vinegar

2 tablespoons *nuoc nam*

Toss the vegetables together in a medium bowl. Heat the water, sugars, vinegar, and *nuoc nam* over medium heat, stirring, until sugar dissolves. Remove from heat and pour over vegetables. Refrigerate until ready to serve.

This will keep for up to 3 days in the refrigerator.

Serves 6

Fresh Coconut Cake

Here's Hoppin' John's classic recipe.

4 large eggs, at room temperature

1 egg yolk

1 cup granulated sugar

1 cup sifted cake flour

2 cups grated fresh coconut

1 ¹/₃ cups heavy cream

1 egg white

2 tablespoons confectioners' sugar (optional)

Grease two 9-inch round cake pans, line them with waxed paper, and grease and flour the paper. Preheat the oven to 350 degrees and set the rack in the lower third of the oven.

Beat the eggs and yolk until doubled in volume. Add the sugar and beat until tripled in volume. Add the flour gradually, folding it in as you do. Fold in 1 cup of the coconut and pour the batter into the pans. Bake until a tester comes out clean, about 25 to 30 minutes. Set aside to cool on racks.

Beat the cream and the egg white together until soft peaks form. Fold in the remaining cup of coconut, and confectioners' sugar to taste.

Just before serving, turn the cakes out and remove the paper. Place one layer on a plate and put about a third of the icing on top. Spread it. Place the second layer on top and ice. Sprinkle the top with more coconut if you care to.

Serves 12

ABOVE, FROM LEFT: *Thai Stuffed Crabs and Green Onion and Corn Fritters; another lowcountry cottage; Fresh Coconut Cake.*

DINNER WITH THE NEIGHBORS

"CREAMY" CORN SOUP • CHARLESTON MIXED

SEAFOOD RAGOUT IN A BROWNED RICE SHELL

MIXED PEPPERS IN OIL AND VINEGAR

ENDIVE SALAD WITH BLACKBERRY VINAIGRETTE

HUGUENOT TORTE

This was a big Saturday-night dinner, so we decided to make several courses instead of our usual single-course-and-dessert meal. Corn was in season so we made a soup with a very creamy texture—but no cream—that can be served hot or cold. Next came a sumptuous seafood ragout presented in a rice shell and accompanied by mixed peppers. This was followed by a simple endive salad with blackberry vinaigrette and finished off with another one of John Taylor's revivals, the Huguenot Torte.

RIGHT: *The table overlooking the beach, set with the first course.*

SULLIVAN'S ISLAND

"Creamy" Corn Soup

*This tasty soup is creamy but contains no cream or milk. It's
also extremely easy to prepare. You'll be surprised.*

2 tablespoons unsalted butter

2 cups thinly sliced leeks, white only

1 cup thinly sliced shallots

6 cups rich chicken stock

3 cups fresh corn kernels, cut and scraped from the cobs

Salt

½ teaspoon white pepper

Paprika

Herb sprigs

Melt the butter in a heavy pot with a tight-fitting lid.
Add the leeks and shallots and toss them in the butter.
Place a sheet of waxed paper over pot before putting on
lid. Sweat, stirring several times, over very low heat until
wilted but not browned, about 15 minutes. Add the stock
and bring to a boil over high heat, then turn back to a
simmer for 15 minutes. Add the corn, return to a simmer,
and cook another 5 minutes. Puree in a food processor or
blender. Strain out and discard the solids. Season the
soup with salt and pepper to taste. Serve warm or chilled
with a dollop of crème fraîche or yogurt, sprinkled with a
little paprika and a sprig of herb if you like.

Serves 8

ABOVE: *Savory and warm corn soup.*
RIGHT: *A favorite pastime—crabbing at low tide.*
BELOW, FROM LEFT: *Wicker porch bench; Mixed
Peppers in Oil and Vinegar; wild "ragged robins";
detail of the moss-covered Boone Haw Slave Cabin, a
nearby historic site.*

Charleston Mixed Seafood Ragout in a Browned Rice Shell.

Charleston Mixed Seafood Ragout in a Browned Rice Shell

The rice shell has to be unmolded rather carefully. If you are not in the mood to fuss, simply put the ragout in an attractive bowl and serve it with plain white rice.

5 tablespoons unsalted butter

1 large garlic clove

1 cup finely chopped celery

1 cup finely chopped green bell pepper

1 cup finely chopped onion

7 tablespoons flour

1 pint shucked oysters, drained, with liquor reserved

1 8-ounce bottle clam juice

1 14-ounce can low-salt chicken broth

$1\frac{1}{2}$ cups water

1 large bay leaf

$\frac{1}{2}$ teaspoon salt

$\frac{1}{2}$ teaspoon coarsely ground black pepper

1 tablespoon margarine

$\frac{1}{4}$ pound peeled and deveined shrimp

$\frac{1}{4}$ pound sea scallops, cut in halves

$\frac{1}{4}$ pound lobster (from a $1\frac{1}{2}$-pound lobster, see Note)

1 pint lump crab meat, picked over

$\frac{1}{4}$ teaspoon Tabasco sauce

Browned Rice Shell (recipe follows)

Melt the butter in a large, heavy skillet and sauté the garlic, celery, bell pepper, and onion until wilted but not browned, about 10 minutes. Sprinkle with 5 tablespoons of the flour and cook, stirring with a spatula, for 5 minutes. Slowly add the oyster liquor, clam juice, broth, and water in small amounts, stirring to incorporate. Add bay leaf, salt, and pepper. Cook over very low heat, stirring occasionally, about 1 hour. (If you are going to make the rice shell, do so now, before finishing the ragout.)

Mash together the margarine and 2 tablespoons of flour. To complete dish, remove bay leaf, raise heat to medium-high, and whisk in flour-margarine mixture a little at the time, simmering until thickened, about 5 minutes. Stir in the seafood and cook for 5 minutes, or until shrimp are just pink. Do not overcook. Stir in Tabasco. Spoon and pour finished ragout into the prepared shell.

Serves 6 to 8

Siesta.

Note: To remove the meat from the lobster shell, plunge a live lobster head first into boiling water and boil just long enough to turn the shell red. You aren't cooking the lobster through, just making it possible to remove the meat easily. Remove lobster and allow to cool long enough to handle. Crack shell and pull meat from the tail and claws and clean. Cut into large chunks to be added to the sauce.

Browned Rice Shell

This is another of Hoppin' John Taylor's resurrected Charleston classics.

> 4 cups long-grain white rice
>
> 10 cups water
>
> 2 teaspoons salt
>
> 4 tablespoons unsalted butter

Combine the rice, water, and salt in a heavy saucepan and boil, uncovered, over medium heat until tender and very soft, about 30 minutes. Turn it out into a colander to drain.

Preheat oven to 425 degrees.

Place the butter in a Dutch oven over low heat. When butter begins to melt, remove the pot from the heat and paint the inside of it all over with the butter, using a pastry brush. Dump the drained rice in and press it down evenly into the pot. Bake for 1 hour to 1 hour 15 minutes, or until a golden crust forms where it touches the pan. Remove and let it rest for a few minutes.

Carefully loosen the edges of the shell all around and invert the Dutch oven onto the platter the ragout is to be served from. If rice does not come out, give the pot a sharp downward thrust. When you remove the Dutch oven, you'll have a golden-crusted mound of rice. With a sharp knife, slice off the top $\frac{1}{4}$ inch of the mound. Scoop out center, leaving about a 1-inch wall all around and on the bottom. It is now ready to receive the seafood ragout.

Mixed Peppers
in Oil and Vinegar

*Obviously this looks best if you can find several
colors of peppers, but if the mixed colors are not available,
use three red and one small green bell pepper.*

1 each red, yellow, orange, and purple sweet pepper

2 tablespoons olive oil

2 teaspoons balsamic vinegar

Salt and black pepper

Seed the peppers and cut into strips. Heat oil over medium-high heat and add peppers. Cook until just crisp-tender, tossing all the while, about 10 to 12 minutes. Sprinkle with the vinegar and then the salt and pepper. Toss to mix.

Serve hot or warm.

Serves 6

Endive Salad
with Blackberry Vinaigrette

*Fruit vinegars are a very good foil for the
slightly sweet-bitter taste of endive.*

6 tablespoons olive oil

3 tablespoons blackberry vinegar

1/2 teaspoon salt

1/4 teaspoon coarsely ground black pepper

1/2 teaspoon Dijon mustard

1 1/2 generous teaspoons minced shallot

6 to 8 large blackberries

5 Belgian endive, separated into spears

Additional blackberries, for garnish (optional)

Whisk together the oil, vinegar, salt, pepper, and mustard. Stir in the shallot and mash in the blackberries.

Place endive spears on individual plates and spoon some of the vinaigrette over each. You could garnish this with another blackberry on each plate and a grind of black pepper.

Serves 6

Huguenot Torte

*Here is another of John Taylor's recipes. He uses a combination
of pecans, walnuts, and black walnuts.*

1 cup mixed nuts

1 good-size apple, peeled and cored

3 large eggs, at room temperature

3/4 cup plus 2 tablespoons sugar

6 tablespoons all-purpose flour

8 pecan halves

Sugar

1/3 cup heavy cream, whipped

Preheat the oven to 375 degrees and put a pan of water in the bottom of the oven. Grease a 9-inch round pan, line it with waxed paper, and grease and flour the paper.

Finely chop the nuts. Very finely chop the apple.

Beat eggs at very high speed until doubled—this may take 10 minutes. Slowly beat in sugar and continue until tripled in volume. Don't be afraid of overbeating.

Sift flour over the mixture. Sprinkle with the nuts, and then the apple. Fold together rapidly but gently, being certain that all elements from the bottom are included.

Pour into the prepared pan and bake in the middle of the oven for 25 to 30 minutes, until the top is golden and has begun to pull away from the sides. Do not press on the top of the cake.

Place the cake on a rack in a draft-free place and allow to cool completely.

While cake is cooling, toast the pecan halves. While they're still hot, dip them quickly in warm water and then roll them in sugar. Allow to cool on a rack.

Turn out the cake and remove waxed paper. Place on a serving plate. Place 8 rosettes or dollops of whipped cream on top of the cake and top each of these with a pecan half.

Serves 8

TOP: *Endive Salad with Blackberry Vinaigrette.* ABOVE: *A traditional Huguenot Torte.*

SUNDAY LUNCH

WARM SHRIMP, WHITE BEAN, AND TOMATO SALAD

JOHN'S BENNE CRACKERS

BLACKBERRY AND PEACH COBBLER

This salad is easy for me to make because I usually have a container of cooked white beans in the refrigerator during the summer. They are a great addition to sandwich or soup lunches. So all we needed to add were the delicious grilled, marinated shrimp and tomatoes. The benne crackers are strictly old lowcountry, and again we used a John Taylor recipe for them. We decided on a real treat for dessert, a cobbler. We got no complaints.

ABOVE: *Lantana.* OPPOSITE: *Warm Shrimp, White Bean, and Tomato Salad, and a plate of John's Benne Crackers.*

Warm Shrimp, White Bean, and Tomato Salad

The marinade gives the shrimp a distinctive flavor. You'll also end up with more beans than you need for the salad, but I like them in composed salads and as a side dish, peppered, dressed with olive oil, and served at room temperature.

BEANS

1 12-ounce bag great northern beans

6 cups chicken stock

2 bay leaves

VINAIGRETTE

2 tablespoons balsamic vinegar

1 generous teaspoon Dijon mustard

$3/4$ teaspoon salt

$1/2$ teaspoon black pepper

5 tablespoons olive oil

3 tablespoons canola oil

SHRIMP

30 large shrimp, peeled and deveined

1 small onion, chopped

1 tablespoon chopped fresh ginger

4 large garlic cloves, mashed

2 large green onions, white and green parts, chopped

$1/2$ cup fresh lemon juice

$1/4$ cup soy sauce

2 tablespoons honey

ASSEMBLY

1 large head Boston lettuce, washed, dried, and cut into
   $1/4$-inch julienne strips

Salt and pepper

$1/4$ cup minced red onion

1 large tomato, peeled, seeded, chopped coarsely,
   and salted

Make the beans. Pick over and soak the beans overnight. Drain and place in a deep pot. Add chicken stock and bay leaves. Bring to a boil quickly and turn heat back. Simmer very slowly, uncovered, until beans are tender, about $1 1/2$ hours. Discard the bay leaves.

Make the vinaigrette. Whisk together the vinegar, mustard, salt, and pepper. Whisk in the oils. Set aside.

Marinate the shrimp. Combine all the ingredients and marinate for 30 minutes. Place the shrimp on skewers.

Assemble the salad. Preheat the broiler. Cover 6 luncheon plates with the lettuce. Sprinkle with a little salt and pepper. Measure out 4 cups of drained beans. (If they are sticking together, place them in a strainer and wash quickly with hot water.) Toss the beans with the red onion and $1/4$ cup of the vinaigrette. Divide beans equally among the plates. Sprinkle tomato cubes over beans, dividing among the plates.

Broil the shrimp for 3 minutes per side. Top each salad with 5 shrimp. Top with a good grind of black pepper and spoon a little of the vinaigrette over the shrimp.

Serves 6

John's Benne Crackers

There are many versions of these, both sweet and savory, but I think John Taylor's is one of the best I've had.

$2 2/3$ cups all-purpose flour

$1 1/2$ teaspoons salt

$1/4$ teaspoon cayenne pepper

$1/2$ cup unsalted butter

$1/2$ cup solid vegetable shortening, chilled

$1/3$ cup ice water

$1 1/3$ cups toasted benne seeds (see Note)

Preheat the oven to 350 degrees. Sift the dry ingredients together. Cut in the butter and shortening until it is evenly distributed and about the size of small peas. Gradually add water until the dough just begins to hold together. You may not need all the water. Mix in the seeds and form into a ball.

Pinch off a piece of dough about the size of a large marble. Roll into a ball and place on a cookie sheet coated with vegetable spray. Flatten with the palm of your hand. Fill out pan and bake until crisped, about 35 to 40 minutes, turning once with a spatula.

Cool and store in an airtight container.

Makes about 36

Note: To toast benne, or sesame, seeds place raw seeds in a single layer on a baking sheet. Roast in a 350 degree oven until golden, about 15 minutes. This may also be done over medium heat in a skillet, stirring often.

OPPOSITE: *In the shade of the arbor.*

Blackberry and Peach Cobbler

By now you must know about me and cobblers. Here's another.

PASTRY

1 1/2 cups all-purpose flour

Pinch of salt

5 tablespoons frozen butter

4 tablespoons frozen solid vegetable shortening

4 to 5 tablespoons ice water

5 large peaches, skinned, pitted, and cut into
   medium slices

2 cups blackberries

1 cup sugar

4 tablespoons unsalted butter

1 cup heavy cream, whipped and flavored with sugar
   and bourbon to taste; or vanilla ice cream

Preheat the oven to 450 degrees. Lightly grease a 1 1/2-
to 2-quart baking dish.

Make the pastry. Pulse flour and salt a couple of times in
the food processor. Add frozen butter and shortening.
Process until shortening is the size of small peas. Add
water and process until dough just holds together. Gather
into a ball and place between 2 sheets of waxed paper.
Flatten into a disc and wrap in paper. Refrigerate for
about 30 minutes.

Roll out pastry on a floured surface into a large ragged
circle. Line the dish, allowing excess to drape over sides.
Toss the peaches and berries together and heap into the
dish, mounding slightly in the center. Pour sugar evenly
over the fruit and dot with the butter. Flop loose ends of
dough over the fruit, using any that break off to patch.

Place in the oven, turn heat back to 425 degrees, and
bake until bubbly and golden, about 45 minutes.

Serve with the whipped cream or vanilla ice cream.

Serves 6 to 8

ABOVE RIGHT AND ABOVE FAR RIGHT: *A typical
large summer "cottage."* RIGHT: *Blackberry and Peach Cobbler.*
FAR RIGHT: *A face full of freckles.*

Tesuque,
New Mexico

OVER THE YEARS SANTA FE (with it's surrounding small communities) has become a haven for artists of all sorts—painters, writers, sculptors—as well as potters, woodworkers, and weavers. Adding a bit of extra zest is a music season that attracts renowned performers, composers, and an ever-increasing audience, some of whom decide to stay. As is typical in such situations, the pretenders in these endeavors far outnumber the truly gifted. But whatever the proportion of real to aspiring talent, there's enough artistic ferment to give the locality a genuine crackle of excitement.

Yet there's still something else. Something harder to define, almost more felt than seen. That something has to do with an American Indian sensibility. In this part of the Southwest the presence of native Americans, and an essential spirituality, is strong. And I believe it's this mystic element as much as the quality of the remarkable, and remarkably changeable and beautiful, landscape that has been such a magnet to creative people.

It's interesting that Santa Fe and its environs were an interconnected—and sometime warring—group of Indian pueblos long before the city became a reality, for to some extent the same thing exists today. The population has dispersed into small groups around the central hub of Santa Fe. These people, often part of the creative community, have moved away from the bustle and commercialization that is the fate of almost all such places as Santa Fe.

Many of these retreats are quite old themselves and are on sites adjoining ancient pueblos—still close enough to Santa Fe to draw on its vitality, yet removed enough to allow its residents to enjoy the great stillness and magical tranquillity that made this area so compelling to begin with.

Two such enclaves are Tesuque, north of the city, and Galisteo, south of the city. They look nothing alike really, but the two areas have a bond that makes them part of a mysterious whole.

The food of the area is as individual as the terrain and architecture, and quite frankly, although I've been enjoying it for some time now, I've not really cooked it much. For that reason I enlisted the help of Priscilla Hoback, a multitalented artist, whose ceramic wall pieces and other works are widely known but whose culinary skills are not, and a young local chef and teacher, Lawrence McGrael. They helped guide me through this distinctive cooking and they were kind enough to share their recipes.

Note: It's important to understand that in recipes from the Southwest, when the list of ingredients calls for chili powder, it does *not* refer to the sort of chili powder usually sold in the markets throughout the rest of the country, which contains not only ground chilies but a number of other ingredients. Chili powder to Southwesterners means ground pure chili peppers and nothing else. In all instances where chili powder is called for the product is pure ground chili pepper.

If pure ground chili powder is not available in your city, you may want to use the mail order sources listed at the back of the book.

Lazy Lunch

Mango Gazpacho with Shrimp and Grapefruit Jalapeño Ice

Double Cheese Tortilla Stacks • Black Bean and Jicama Salad

Ricotta Espresso Torte

Now, this is the kind of lunch I enjoy. It's basically uncomplicated and easy to prepare (I'm assuming you'll make the dessert in advance), but it has a few nice surprises, like the mango gazpacho with shrimp and grapefruit jalapeño ice.

Tortilla stacks couldn't be simpler, and when you serve them along with a bean salad (and maybe a little of that salsa you have waiting in your refrigerator), you've got quite a tasty combination. The dessert is sinful, of course, and you'll have enough left over to sin again. It's one specialty of local dessert expert Ann Minty, bless her sugar-coated heart.

ABOVE: *Bright helianthus.* OPPOSITE: *Easy lunch in the garden shade.*

Mango Gazpacho with Shrimp and Grapefruit Jalapeño Ice

This fresh-tasting gazpacho may be made the day before. The recipe may look complicated, but the only actual cooking is the shrimp, which take a brief few minutes—so the whole thing is actually quite undemanding. The grapefruit jalapeño ice that garnishes the soup is a nice touch of surprising flavor, but you could leave it off if you're in a rush.

This imaginative recipe came to us from chef Lawrence McGrael.

GAZPACHO

1/4 cup fresh orange juice

Juice of 2 limes

3 large ripe mangoes, peeled, seeded, and pureed

2 tablespoons finely chopped fresh cilantro

2 tablespoons finely chopped cucumbers

2 tablespoons finely chopped red bell pepper

2 tablespoons finely chopped red onion

2 teaspoons Oriental sesame oil

1 tablespoon rice wine vinegar

1/2 teaspoon salt

1/4 teaspoon black pepper

SHRIMP

18 medium shrimp, peeled and deveined

1 bay leaf

2 tablespoons olive oil

1 tablespoon fresh lime juice

Salt

Grapefruit Jalapeño Ice (recipe follows)

Make the gazpacho. Stir the orange and lime juices into the mango puree. Stir in all other ingredients. Cover and chill.

Prepare the shrimp. Bring about 5 cups water to a boil and add shrimp, bay leaf, and 1 tablespoon of the oil. Bring back to a boil and cook until pink, about 2 to 3 minutes.

Drain, and toss with the remaining oil and lime juice. Sprinkle with salt to taste. Cool and refrigerate, covered.

To serve, divide gazpacho into 6 individual bowls, float 3 shrimp on each serving, and top with a cube of the ice.

Serves 6

Grapefruit Jalapeño Ice

1/2 cup sugar

1 cup fresh grapefruit juice (2 medium)

4 teaspoons minced jalapeño pepper (about 1 1/2 medium)

Scant teaspoon minced fresh cilantro

Dissolve the sugar in the grapefruit juice. Stir in other ingredients. Pour into ice tray, preferably metal, and freeze. To remove the ice, run a knife around sides of each cube and lift out with a fork or the knife.

Double Cheese Tortilla Stacks

These are sort of a Mexican-Southwestern version of toasted cheese sandwiches—and you know how everyone loves those. They are a snap to make and invite innovation. Incidentally, if the top tortilla should cook too quickly and become too crisp, simply turn the stack over when it's done and press down lightly to flatten it out; then cut with the crisp side down.

9 ounces muenster or Monterey jack cheese, shredded

9 6-inch flour tortillas

6 tablespoons minced red onion

6 tablespoons minced, drained canned mild chili peppers

9 ounces cheddar, asiago, or fontina cheese, shredded

Black pepper

Place a baking sheet in the oven and preheat to 450 degrees.

Divide the shredded muenster cheese among 3 of the tortillas, leaving about 1/2 inch bare around the edges. Sprinkle each with 1 tablespoon of the minced onion and chili pepper. Cover with another tortilla. This time top the tortilla with the cheddar and the balance of the minced onion and chili pepper. Sprinkle with a little pepper. Top each stack with a third tortilla.

Carefully slide the tortilla stacks onto the heated baking sheet. Bake until edges are toasted and the cheese has melted, about 10 minutes. Remove with a spatula. Allow to cool for about a minute and cut each stack into 4 wedges. Serve 2 wedges per guest.

Serves 6

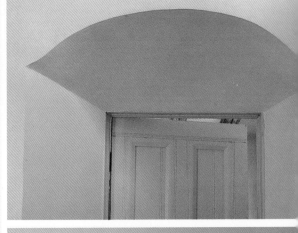

ABOVE LEFT: *Fenced approach to the house.* TOP TO BOTTOM: *Back garden gate; detail of a deep door reveal; typical brick mantel.* LEFT: *Mango Gazpacho with Shrimp and Grapefruit Jalapeño Ice.* OVERLEAF, FROM LEFT: *End of the rainbow; view toward the side patio; collection of bleached stag horns.*

Black Bean and Jicama Salad and Double Cheese Tortilla Stacks.

Black Bean and Jicama Salad

*The proportion of ingredients added to the beans is
fairly flexible, so feel free to add or subtract after you taste this.*

BEANS

2 cups dried black beans, soaked and drained

6 cups cold water

¾ teaspoon salt

½ teaspoon black pepper

¾ teaspoon ground cumin

1 bay leaf

VINAIGRETTE

2 tablespoons red wine vinegar

1 teaspoon Dijon mustard

¾ teaspoon salt, or to taste

¼ teaspoon black pepper

6 tablespoons olive oil

ASSEMBLY

1 cup peeled and diced medium-small jicama

1 medium tomato, cored and seeded, medium chopped

¼ cup green onions cut into small rings, with some green

2 tablespoons minced fresh cilantro

Cook the beans. Put all the ingredients together in a pot and bring to a boil over high heat. Turn back to a slow boil and cook until tender, about 50 minutes. Remove from heat and allow to cool to room temperature. Remove bay leaf.

Make the vinaigrette. Combine the vinegar, mustard, and salt and pepper. Whisk in the oil. Set aside at room temperature.

Assemble the salad. Toss the remaining ingredients together with the beans. Add 5 or 6 tablespoons of the vinaigrette and toss again. Use all the vinaigrette if you need it, but do this by taste.

Serves 6 to 8

Ricotta Espresso Torte.

Ricotta Espresso Torte

*This is made with homemade round ladyfinger layers.
And it's actually better if it's made the day before you serve it.*

LADYFINGER LAYERS
5 large eggs, separated
¾ cup sugar
1 tablespoon vanilla extract
¾ cup all-purpose flour

CARAMEL
1 cup sugar
¼ cup water

FILLING
3 large egg yolks
¼ cup espresso coffee
¼ cup sugar
2 tablespoons Kahlúa
2 tablespoons vanilla extract
1¼ cups ricotta cheese
1 cup heavy cream, whipped

ASSEMBLY
2 tablespoons sugar
2 tablespoons instant coffee granules
½ cup fresh-brewed coffee
Sugar for sprinkling

Make the ladyfinger layers. Preheat oven to 350 degrees. Grease and flour 3 baking sheets.

With a hand mixer, beat the egg whites until foamy. Add ½ cup sugar a little at a time while continuing to beat until soft peaks form. Set aside.

With a hand mixer, beat the yolks and the remaining ¼ cup of sugar until light and frothy. Beat in the vanilla.

Beat in flour a few tablespoons at a time. Fold in the reserved whites, a third at a time.

Make 3 equal mounds of the batter on the prepared baking sheets and spread out into 9-inch circles. Bake until light golden and centers spring back when touched. Allow to cool.

Make the caramel. Cover a baking sheet with lightly oiled foil and set aside.

Combine sugar and water in a heavy saucepan. Stir. Bring to a boil over medium-high heat, brushing any sugar crystals from the sides of the pan with a pastry brush dipped in water. Continue to boil until mixture turns a cola brown. Carefully pour the caramel onto the prepared sheet and allow it to harden. When hard, peel off the foil and smash the caramel into small nuggets with a hammer or meat tenderizer. Set aside.

Make the filling. Place yolks, espresso, sugar, Kahlúa, and vanilla in a nonreactive saucepan over medium heat and whisk until frothy and tripled in volume. Transfer to a mixing bowl and beat with a hand mixer until cool, about 5 minutes. Add ricotta cheese and beat until smooth. Gently fold in the whipped cream.

Assemble the torte. Mix the sugar and coffee granules. Have the brewed coffee ready with a brush.

Lightly oil a 9-inch springform pan and sprinkle with sugar. Place one of the ladyfinger layers in the bottom and brush with some of the coffee. Spoon just under half the ricotta filling onto the layer and smooth it out. Place another of the circles on and brush with coffee. Spoon on most of the remaining filling and smooth it. Sprinkle with some of the caramelized sugar nuggets and part of the coffee-sugar mixture. Place the last layer on and again brush with coffee. Smooth the remaining filling into a thin layer on top and sprinkle with the rest of the caramel and the sugar-coffee mixture.

Wrap securely with plastic wrap and place in the freezer for at least 4 hours.

Remove the torte from the pan and transfer it to the refrigerator. Serve chilled but not frozen.

Serves 10 to 12

BUFFET PARTY IN GALISTEO

BAKED CHILI RELLENOS • BLUE CORN ENCHILADAS • PINTO BEANS

COUNTRY-STYLE SPARE RIBS • CHOPPED CELERY, APPLE, AND PEAR SALAD

FRESH CORN SALSA • PEARS

Through mutual friends, I met a fascinating artist named Priscilla Hoback. Priscilla lives and has her studio in the tiny village of Galisteo, about thirty minutes outside Santa Fe. It turns out she is not only an exceptionally gifted artist but an exceptionally good cook who comes by her culinary skills naturally; her mother is the moving force behind the renowned Pink Adobe Restaurant.

Anyway, I asked her if she would make some traditional dishes for us, and she came up with a feast! Like many other cooks of the region, Priscilla usually has things on hand that the ordinary cook might not keep at the ready, such as the chili sauces she uses. However, these are so delicious and potentially have such varied uses, maybe it's time we all started considering keeping a supply of such flexible additives in our refrigerators.

The menu obviously includes many more dishes than needed for an ordinary gathering, but I think you'll find plenty here to build other meals around. For instance, either the relleños, the enchiladas, or the ribs with a salad would make a fine supper menu.

Incidentally, Priscilla often serves good, strong, fresh lemonade with meals, the flavor of which is as compatible with the spicy dishes of the region as iced tea is with the Southern meals I grew up with.

OPPOSITE: *Noted sculptress and ceramicist Priscilla Hoback.*

Baked Chili Relleños

In most kitchens stuffed mild green chili peppers are filled and fried. I like Priscilla's version, which does away with the frying.

24 fresh mild green chili peppers

Vegetable oil

1 cup diced onion

½ cup golden raisins

1 cup fresh yellow corn kernels, cut from the cob

½ cup pine nuts

1¼ cups shredded mozzarella cheese

1¼ cups shredded cheddar cheese

4 large eggs, lightly beaten

½ teaspoon salt

Few dashes Maggi seasoning

4 tablespoons unsalted butter, melted

1 cup evaporated skim milk

¼ teaspoon black pepper

1 teaspoon minced fresh oregano, or ½ teaspoon dried

Preheat the oven to 450 degrees. Rub peppers with vegetable oil and place on a baking sheet. Cook until skin begins to blister, about 10 to 15 minutes. Place in a brown paper bag and fold shut. Allow to cool.

Meanwhile, place a heavy skillet over high heat and when it is very hot add the onion (no oil). Do not stir. When the onion begins to caramelize start shaking the pan from time to time. When well caramelized remove to a bowl.

Lightly grease a 2-quart casserole. Rub skins off the peppers and split each in half, removing seeds. Place one-third of the halves in a layer on the bottom of the casserole. Sprinkle with a third of the onion, raisins, corn, and pine nuts. Combine the cheeses and sprinkle a third if it over the onion. Repeat to make 3 layers, finishing with the cheese.

Preheat the oven to 350 degrees.

Mix the remaining ingredients and pour over the layered peppers. Stir slightly to make sure it gets under the bottom layer.

Bake, covered, for 30 minutes. Remove cover and bake another 30 minutes or until set and cheese is bubbly.

Serves 6

RIGHT: *Priscilla's bounty.*

Blue Corn Enchiladas

This recipe calls for a red chili sauce,
which is one of the things Priscilla always has on hand.

RED CHILI SAUCE

15 to 18 dried hot red chili peppers

$\frac{1}{4}$ cup olive oil

1 large head of garlic, cut in half

1 pound ground beef shoulder

1 cup pure chili powder

1 teaspoon salt

1 tablespoon flour

1 quart chicken stock

$\frac{1}{2}$ teaspoon dried oregano

$\frac{1}{2}$ teaspoon ground cumin

ASSEMBLY

1 dozen blue corn tortillas

Vegetable oil

$\frac{1}{4}$ cup caramelized onions (follow method in instructions for Baked Chili Relleños, page 46)

1 cup shredded cheddar cheese

1 cup shredded Monterey jack cheese

Mild goat or farmer cheese, for garnish

Make the sauce. Under running water, split dried peppers and wash out seeds. Cover with hot water and soak for 10 to 15 minutes.

Meanwhile, heat the oil in a large, heavy skillet over medium-high heat and sauté the garlic for a minute. Add the meat and chili powder and fry till very brown, stirring all the while, about 8 to 10 minutes. Stir in the salt and flour.

Drain the peppers and puree them in a processor to make a smooth paste.

Add the chicken stock to the meat and bring to a simmer. Add the pepper puree and seasonings. Bring to a boil, then turn back to a simmer, reducing until thickened (like tomato sauce), about 20 minutes.

Assemble. Preheat the oven to 350 degrees. Lightly oil a 14-inch oval casserole.

Warm the tortillas in a very lightly oiled heavy pan over high heat, turning once, until soft, about 30 seconds per side.

Fill each tortilla with $\frac{1}{4}$ cup of the chili sauce and a teaspoon of the caramelized onion. Mix the cheddar and jack and divide $1\frac{1}{2}$ cups evenly among the tortillas. Roll the enchiladas and place seam side down in the casserole. Pour the remaining cup of sauce over the enchiladas and sprinkle with the remaining $\frac{1}{2}$ cup of cheese. Bake uncovered for 30 minutes or until bubbly. Sprinkle with crumbled cheese before serving.

Serves 6

Pinto Beans

As most everyone knows, pinto beans in one form or another are a staple of the Southwestern diet. Of course, in New Orleans beans are simply red beans, the basis for that favorite Louisiana dish, red beans and rice.

2 cups dried pinto beans, soaked overnight and drained

2 cups water

1 pound ham hock, roughly cut

1 teaspoon dried oregano

1 teaspoon ground cumin

1 tablespoon pure chili powder

1 teaspoon salt

Place the drained beans in a pot along with the other ingredients.

Bring to a boil, reduce to a simmer, and cook, skimming, until tender, $2\frac{1}{2}$ to 3 hours. Add more water if needed to keep beans covered.

Serves 6 to 8

Golden pears for dessert.

TOP: *Priscilla's studio.* ABOVE: *Exercising the horses.*

49

Country-Style Spare Ribs

These are almost a meal in themselves.

10 country-cut spare ribs
1 large onion, sliced thin
3 tablespoons pure chili powder
3 medium garlic cloves, minced
$\frac{1}{2}$ cup chopped celery
2 cups Red Chili Sauce (page 48)

Place ribs in a large pot and cover with water. Bring to a boil, reduce to a simmer, and cook for 30 minutes to remove some of the fat.

Preheat the oven to 300 degrees.

Drain the ribs and place in a roasting pan. Sprinkle with all the seasonings and aromatics and top with 1 cup of the chili sauce. Bake, basting with the pan juices every 30 minutes or so. After 1$\frac{1}{2}$ hours, add the remaining cup of chili sauce. Bake until meat is tender and falling off the bone, 2$\frac{1}{2}$ to 3 hours.

Serves 8 to 10

Chopped Celery, Apple, and Pear Salad

*The sweet crunchy flavor of this salad is just the
right foil for the other hot dishes.*

3 cups thinly sliced celery
2 large Granny Smith apples, peeled, cored, and
    sliced thin
2 large Bosc pears, peeled, cored, and sliced thin
1 medium garlic clove, cut in half
$\frac{1}{2}$ teaspoon salt
$\frac{1}{4}$ cup olive oil
$\frac{1}{4}$ cup fresh raspberries
$\frac{1}{4}$ cup fresh orange juice
2 tablespoons raspberry vinegar

Toss the celery, apples, and pears together in a bowl. Place all other ingredients in a food processor and process until smooth. Toss with the celery and fruit. Chill, covered, for 1 hour before serving.

Serves 8

Fresh Corn Salsa

This salsa is good with almost anything!

2 cups yellow corn kernels, freshly cut from the cob
4 tablespoons unsalted butter
$\frac{1}{2}$ cup evaporated skim milk
1 small white onion, coarsely chopped
1 medium garlic clove, coarsely chopped
3 ripe medium tomatoes, cored and roughly chopped
1 medium jalapeño pepper, cut in half and seeded
2 to 3 mild green chili peppers, cut in half and seeded

Combine corn, butter, and milk in a small saucepan over high heat, stirring. When it comes to a boil, reduce heat and simmer 2 minutes. Set aside.

Combine all other ingredients in a food processor and chop to a coarse consistency. Stir into corn. May be served warm or at room temperature.

This should not be made too far in advance.

Makes about 3 cups

ABOVE: *Crabapples on the vine.*
OPPOSITE: *Detail of a nearby church.*

Orcas Island, Washington

THE ISLANDS AROUND SEATTLE are called the San Juans, and they are actually the tops of an ancient mountain range that was flooded as the last great glacial age came to a close. It's probably not worth trying to puzzle out how many islands there are in this group because the total will vary according to where you draw the boundaries—and even how you define *island*. But it's safe to say that there are at least 170 large enough to be inhabited by more than just native squirrels and deer, even if this human habitation is nothing more than a single rustic cabin with a boat dock.

Each large island has its own particular charm and character, but all are generously forested and rocky with a myriad of quiet coves—and all share truly extravagant vistas of neighboring islands and open water.

Orcas is one of those islands that takes a bit of doing to reach, and it can be a fairly long journey from Seattle. To go by car ferry, one has to get to Anacortes (itself on an island), several hours' drive north of Seattle. I'm told in the summer one should plan to be in line a couple of hours early to get on the ferry. Once on board, however, the sleek carriers give you a glorious hour-plus ride with those vistas to greet you on every side.

Of all the larger islands, Orcas, with its tall mountains and deep inlets, has traditionally been a favored recreation spot, even during an earlier period when its residents were busy with agriculture and the marine industry. Legend has it that the Lummi Indians who claimed Orcas as part of their tribal territory summered here where berries and other favored foodstuffs were plentiful and the weather cool. Actually these islands must have provided an idyllic retreat, with so much natural bounty from the sea and land.

Well, happily, there are still plenty of berries, shellfish, and those cool breezes. Today, if you are in the mood, there is also camping, hiking, and tennis as well as part of a national park and a bird sanctuary to explore. With a bicycle and good legs, one can cover the island in a day. And if you've got friends with a house, you can laze around and cook, after you've had your fill of whichever of these activities you like.

Luckily, we had friends with a house.

PRECEDING PAGES: *Late evening on the bay.* ABOVE: *A local church.* OPPOSITE: *One last stroll on the dock.*

DINNER ON THE TERRACE

SWEET RED PEPPER ASPIC • CELERY ROOT REMOULADE

TOAST • BAKED THIN-SLICED SALMON

WARM COUSCOUS-STUFFED TOMATOES • BLACKBERRY MOUSSE

Of course, the salmon one gets in Washington State is great, so we decided to include it in several meals. Here, thin slices are marinated and then quickly cooked in the oven. It's not a new technique, but it's one that many chefs use because it is so fast. You might try it with other firm-textured fish.

To go with the fish are couscous-stuffed tomatoes—scrumptious. And to start the meal is a composed first course: a slice of sweet red pepper aspic and celery root rémoulade. Blackberries are another abundant local ingredient, so we made a mousse using them. Of course by the time we arrived the season was finished, but we used local frozen ones, which worked just fine in this recipe. And since the day was warm we dined out on the terrace overlooking the sound.

ABOVE: *Split log fence.* OPPOSITE: *Sweet Red Pepper Aspic, Celery Root Rémoulade, and some crisp toast.*

Sweet Red Pepper Aspic

*By now, many of you know how I
am about aspics. Here's another—and it's good.*

5 tablespoons water

2 envelopes unflavored gelatin

2 tablespoons unsalted butter

2 tablespoons olive oil

2¼ cups coarsely chopped red onions

2 medium garlic cloves, minced

3 very large red bell peppers, roasted, peeled, seeded,
 and chopped

2 cups chicken stock

Salt and pepper

Mayonnaise, preferably homemade

Put water in a small saucer and sprinkle the gelatin
over it; let the gelatin dissolve.

Heat the butter and oil in a large skillet over medium-
high heat and sauté the onion until lightly browned,
about 5 minutes. Add the garlic and cook another
minute. Add the peppers, stock, salt, and pepper. Pour
into a processor and process until smooth. Transfer to a
bowl and stir in the gelatin, stirring until dissolved. Pour
into a ring mold and refrigerate until set, about 3 hours.

To serve, place the mold in a bowl of hot water for a
few seconds, just long enough to loosen it. Place the
serving plate over it and invert. Refrigerate until melted
gelatin sets again. Serve with a dab of mayonnaise.

Serves 8 or more

Celery Root Rémoulade

*Although I envisioned this as part of a first course, it could be
served with the entree as a side dish.*

2 tablespoons Creole or brown mustard (see Sources)

1 tablespoon paprika

½ teaspoon salt

¼ cup cider vinegar

2 medium garlic cloves, coarsely chopped

¼ cup finely chopped celery

¼ cup minced fresh parsley

¼ cup minced green onions

2 tablespoons mayonnaise

2 large celery roots

Juice of 1 lemon

Place the mustard, paprika, salt, vinegar, and garlic in a
processor and process until smooth. Pour into a bowl and
stir in the remaining ingredients, except celery roots and
lemon juice.

Peel the celery roots and cut into ¼-inch julienne.
Cover with water in a small saucepan and add the lemon
juice. Simmer until tender, 1 to 2 minutes. Drain and dry.
Combine with enough sauce to coat well and refrigerate.

Serves 6 or more

ABOVE: *Flotilla of geese.* ABOVE
RIGHT: *Looking in through the house.*
RIGHT: *Baked Thin-Sliced Salmon and
Warm Couscous-Stuffed Tomatoes.*
BELOW LEFT: *View across the bay.*
BELOW: *Washington State apples.*

Baked Thin-Sliced Salmon

I'm very partial to this method of cooking salmon. You can even do it directly on the dinner plates if they are ovenproof.

1/2 cup fresh dill, no stems

1/4 cup fresh lemon juice

1/2 cup olive oil

3 tablespoons Dijon mustard

1 1 1/2- to 2-pound salmon filet, in 1 piece

Combine all ingredients but the salmon in a food processor and process until smooth. This will have the consistency of mayonnaise.

Wrap the salmon in plastic and put in the freezer for 10 minutes. Unwrap and cut at an angle against the grain into 1/4-inch-thick slices—as if you were slicing smoked salmon. This should give you 12 slices.

Place slices in a dish and combine with the marinade, making sure all surfaces are coated. Cover and marinate 4 to 6 hours, refrigerated.

Preheat the oven to 450 degrees. Coat 2 baking sheets with vegetable spray and arrange 6 slices on each. Smooth the marinade with a spatula. Bake in the center of the oven for 2 1/2 to 3 minutes, until flaky. Remove to warmed plates with a spatula. May be garnished with fresh herbs or lemon.

Serves 6

Warm Couscous-Stuffed Tomatoes

The trick here is not to cook these so long that they fall apart.

6 medium tomatoes, about 1/2 pound each

2 tablespoons olive oil

6 tablespoons minced onion

3/4 cup minced red bell pepper

2 tablespoons coarsely chopped fresh parsley

2 1/2 cups couscous cooked in chicken stock

Salt and pepper

Preheat the oven to 350 degrees.

Cut off a slice from the top of each tomato and use a grapefruit knife to clean out all pulp. Be careful to leave the wall of the tomato intact. Reserve the pulp and invert the tomato shells onto a paper towel.

Place oil in a large skillet and sauté the onion and red pepper until wilted, about 5 minutes. Add 1 cup plus 2 tablespoons of the reserved tomato pulp. Cook over medium-high heat to reduce for about 10 minutes. Stir in parsley and couscous. Season well with salt and pepper.

Rub the inside of each tomato with salt and pepper and heap the couscous mixture into each, mounding the tops. Coat a pan just large enough to hold the 6 tomatoes tightly with vegetable spray and place them in. Bake until heated through, about 15 minutes. If you overcook them they will split and collapse, so keep an eye on them.

Serves 6

Blackberry Mousse

You could use other berries for this or even a combination of several kinds. And you can always try it with fresh berries.

1 pound frozen blackberries

1 cup sugar

2 tablespoons fresh lemon juice

2 tablespoons water

1 envelope unflavored gelatin

1 cup heavy cream, whipped

4 large egg whites, beaten until stiff but not dry

Fresh mint, for garnish

Combine berries, sugar, and lemon juice in a nonreactive saucepan. Bring to a boil over medium heat. Remove from heat and allow to cool. Puree and set aside.

Put the water in a small saucer and sprinkle the gelatin over it. Set aside for a few minutes.

Stir the softened gelatin into the berry puree. Fold in the whipped cream. Fold in the beaten egg whites. Place in individual goblets or in a soufflé dish and refrigerate for at least 1 hour before serving.

Serve garnished with fresh mint, accompanied by cookies if you like.

Serves 8

TOP: *Dinner after a cruise.* ABOVE: *Blackberry Mousse.*

Dinner in Front of the Fire

PASTA WITH CHEVRE, SMOKED SALMON, AND CORN

FOCACCIA • SIMPLE SALAD

RUM CHERRY ICE CREAM

One day it suddenly turned very cold and blustery as it can do here in the early fall, so we figured dinner in front of the fire would be just the ticket.

We decided to utilize more of that local salmon and some of the luscious local dried cherries. The salmon went into pasta along with the end-of-the-season corn. This was accompanied by an easy focaccia, which we also nibbled along with the green salad.

Chilly weather notwithstanding, we finished with homemade rum cherry ice cream.

ABOVE: *Rum Cherry Ice Cream.* OPPOSITE: *Pasta by the fire.*

Pasta with Chèvre, Smoked Salmon, and Corn

I know that a lot of people like to make creamy cheese-based sauces with reduced heavy cream, but I don't do that any longer. I use evaporated skim milk instead.

6 tablespoons minced red onion

$\frac{1}{4}$ cup olive oil

$\frac{1}{2}$ teaspoon salt or to taste

$1\frac{1}{2}$ cups evaporated skim milk

8 ounces mild chèvre, crumbled

$1\frac{1}{2}$ teaspoons Tabasco sauce

1 pound rotini pasta

1 tablespoon grated lemon rind

$\frac{1}{2}$ teaspoon lemon pepper

12 large basil leaves, cut into strips

6 large mint leaves cut into strips

3 ears white corn kernels, cut from the cob ($1\frac{1}{2}$ to $1\frac{3}{4}$ cups)

10 ounces smoked salmon, cut into large pea-size pieces or flaked, all bones out

GARNISH

6 basil leaves, cut into strips

3 mint leaves, cut into strips

In a medium skillet, wilt the onion in the olive oil over medium heat without browning, stirring, about 5 minutes. Add the salt and milk and heat. Add the cheese and Tabasco and continue to cook over medium heat, stirring, until thick and smooth. Remove from heat.

Put pasta on to cook and when it's almost done, reheat the sauce. Stir in the lemon rind, lemon pepper, basil, mint, and corn.

When pasta is done, drain and place in a warm bowl. Mix salmon into the sauce and pour half over the pasta, tossing. Divide among 6 to 8 individual warmed plates. Place a large spoonful of the sauce on each and sprinkle with strips of basil and mint.

Serves 6 to 8

Focaccia

Focaccia toppings can be as simple or as complicated as you like. Do a little experimenting.

1 package active dry yeast

1 tablespoon sugar

1 cup warm water

1 teaspoon salt

$\frac{1}{4}$ cup plus 1 tablespoon olive oil

3 cups all-purpose flour

Coarse salt

$\frac{1}{2}$ cup thinly sliced red onion

1 teaspoon finely chopped fresh rosemary

In large mixing bowl, dissolve the yeast and sugar in the water. Set aside. When foamy, add salt and $\frac{1}{4}$ cup olive oil. Stir. Mix in 2 cups of the flour with a wooden spoon to make a very sticky dough. Work in the balance of the flour a little at a time with your hands, until all is used and a smooth dough is formed. Knead in a mixer or on a floured board until smooth and elastic. Turn into a lightly oiled bowl and cover with a tea towel. Allow to double in bulk in a warm draft-free spot, about $1\frac{1}{2}$ hours.

Oil a 9-inch square pan. Punch down the dough and pat it evenly into the oiled pan. Cover and allow to rise for another 30 minutes.

Preheat the oven to 450 degrees.

After the dough has risen the second time, poke it with your finger in about 12 different places. Brush with 1 tablespoon olive oil, allowing some to collect in the holes. Sprinkle with coarse salt, red onion, and rosemary.

Bake until golden brown, about 40 minutes. Cut into 4 strips and cut each of these in half. Serve hot with extra olive oil for dipping if desired.

Serves 8

OPPOSITE: *Local flowers on the mantel.*

Simple Salad

Use this dressing on an assortment of your favorite well-washed greens. Serve it with a wedge of cheese if you like.

3 tablespoons canola oil

6 tablespoons olive oil

3 tablespoons red wine vinegar

1 teaspoon grainy Dijon mustard

$\frac{1}{2}$ teaspoon salt

$\frac{1}{2}$ teaspoon black pepper

2 tablespoons minced shallots

Whisk all ingredients but the shallots together. Stir in shallots after vinaigrette is combined.

Makes about $\frac{3}{4}$ cup, enough for 8 generous servings

Rum Cherry Ice Cream

We used Chukar dried cherries for this dessert (see Sources). The company offers a number of varieties of cherries, as well as dried blueberries and cranberries.

$\frac{3}{4}$ cup dried cherries

Light rum

2$\frac{1}{2}$ cups half-and-half

$\frac{1}{2}$ cup sugar

4 large egg yolks

$\frac{1}{4}$ teaspoon vanilla extract

Place the cherries in a bowl and cover with rum. Allow to soak for several hours.

Heat the half-and-half and sugar together until sugar is dissolved and bubbles begin to form around edge of the pot. Whisk yolks until creamy and then whisk in $\frac{1}{2}$ cup of the heated half-and-half mixture. Pour the warmed yolks back into the half-and-half and continue to cook, stirring, until the custard mixture coats the back of a spoon. Do not overcook or the custard will curdle. Stir in vanilla, allow to cool completely, then chill.

Pour into a commercial ice-cream maker and freeze according to manufacturer's directions. Drain the cherries. When the mixture begins to thicken as it freezes, add the cherries and freeze until ice cream is the proper consistency.

Makes about 1$\frac{3}{4}$ pints

Mendocino,

California

PERCHED ON CLIFFS OVERLOOKING a bay formed at the convergence of several rivers flowing into the Pacific, Mendocino has retained a large measure of its original small-town personality and appearance. It looks in some ways like a New England village placed along one of the most spectacularly beautiful stretches of coastline north of San Francisco. Its unassuming buildings—a few topped by spires—line irregular streets with riotously blooming plants overflowing fences and spilling onto uneven sidewalks.

On the drive north from San Francisco to Mendocino, after you turn off near Cloverdale and head toward the coast, you pass through an absolutely glorious stand of fine old redwoods. When I remarked to a local resident what a grand and lovely passageway the redwoods created, she responded rather dryly that that's exactly what this stand of ancients is. When you view it from the air, you see where lumber companies have cleverly left strips of great trees along traveled highways to create the illusion that one is proceeding through a forest.

It was the redwoods that brought "civilization" to this area in the first place—redwoods and a shipwreck. The story goes that sometime around 1851, a ship carrying cargo from China foundered on the rocks a few miles north of what is now Mendocino. The crew brought back word of the extensive redwood forests in the vicinity, so it wasn't long before the race was on to exploit what seemed to be an inexhaustible supply of prime quality wood.

By 1860 the village's population had swelled to 150 whites, with an encampment of about 300 Indians nearby. But Mendocino's greatest population increase came about toward the last quarter of the nineteenth century. Since then it's settled down to percolate quietly, nestled in remarkable scenic grandeur. The town's seen hunters, squatters, hippies, artists, and tourists. It's seen modern bridges built and has had broad highways zip by it. It's had good times and bum times, but nothing seems to bother the place too much.

So here Mendocino is today, sometimes heavy with visitors on special weekends, but still the quiet, secluded spot it's always been.

PRECEDING PAGES: *Mendocino on the cliffs—as the fog lifts.*
ABOVE: *Pacific coast wildflowers.*
OPPOSITE: *Masonic temple cupola.*

BREAKFAST WITH THE NEIGHBORS

MIXED FRUIT CUP • WILD SOURDOUGH PANCAKES

WALNUT HONEY BUTTER • BERRY HONEY • CIDER HAM FINGERS

I bet almost everyone's favorite special treat breakfast is something like pancakes or waffles. Pancakes were our choice for this meal, and I had a recipe for pancakes that was given to me by a friend. To go with the pancakes we made a quick berry honey and some honey-nut butter with local walnuts. Both of these were done the day before so we could get right at the breakfast. Accompanying the pancakes was ham marinated in apple cider, then grilled. Of course, this being California, the local fruit was a delight—so that's what we had for starters.

Incidentally, the neighbor's house is set in the middle of a spectacular garden landscaped with wild grasses and beautiful mounds of heather and lavender. It was spectacular as the sun began to burn off the ocean mist.

ABOVE: *Mixed Fruit Cup.* OPPOSITE: *Wild Sourdough Pancakes, Walnut Honey Butter, Cider Ham Fingers, and a glass of Berry Honey.*

Mixed Fruit Cup

Of course, this may be sweetened if you like.

Use almost any combination of fruit for this breakfast starter. Personally I prefer "soft" fruit for it and avoid harder fruit such as apples and pears. Here we combined orange and grapefruit segments with sliced bananas, kiwis, huckleberries, and a few raspberries left over from making the berry honey.

Citrus fruit should be peeled and the pith scraped off before it is sliced. If pith is stubborn, dip the peeled fruit in boiling water for just a few seconds to make it easier to clean.

To finish, toss the fruit together and pour the juice of one large orange over it all. Refrigerate, covered. If you don't intend to eat this within an hour, leave the banana out; slice it in just before serving.

Wild Sourdough Pancakes

This recipe came to me from Cassandra Mitchell, who owns the popular Diner Restaurant in Yountville, California. Cassandra had it from her grandmother, Jane Grosfield of Big Timber Mountain.

The cakes have a distinctive flavor and lightness. The preparation sounds complicated, but it is simplicity itself. It just takes time.

2 cups all-purpose flour

2 cups warm water

1/2 cup Wild Sourdough Starter (recipe follows)

3 large eggs

4 tablespoons butter, melted

2 tablespoons sugar

1 teaspoon salt

1 1/2 teaspoons baking soda

The night before you make the pancakes, combine the flour, warm water, and starter until blended and smooth (do *not* use a metal spoon or bowl). Cover with a cloth and set aside in a warm place.

Make a batter by stirring in all the other ingredients, mixing well but not hard. Cook on a hot, lightly greased griddle. Let bubbles form on top before turning. If batter seems too thick, thin with a little milk.

Serves 4 to 6

Wild Sourdough Starter

This isn't a formal recipe—just a description. Start this process when you have time to play with it.

In a glass jar or crockery bowl, mix 1 cup all-purpose flour with enough water to make a thick paste that is still on the runny side. Set the jar out uncovered on the counter or the porch to let it start fermenting. It will bubble and start to smell beerlike after a couple of days. Once it does, you're ready to go with the pancakes.

Walnut Honey Butter

As I said earlier, we used good California walnuts for this, but you could use any kind of nut you like, or a combination. We didn't toast the walnuts, but if you use pecans or almonds, their flavor will be improved by toasting.

1/2 cup unsalted butter, softened

1/2 cup finely chopped walnuts

1/4 cup honey

Beat all ingredients together and refrigerate until ready to serve.

Makes 1 generous cup

Berry Honey

It's really better to use frozen berries for this because they're usually cheaper. Besides, you cook them, and the flavor, not the texture, is what counts.

1 generous cup frozen raspberries, strawberries, or blueberries

1 1/2 cups honey

1/4 cup water

1 teaspoon or more grated lemon rind (optional)

Combine the berries, 1/2 cup of the honey, and water in a small saucepan. Simmer over low heat for about 15 minutes. Stir in the balance of the honey. Allow to cool, then stir in optional lemon rind.

Makes about 2 1/2 cups

TOP: *The breakfast table.* ABOVE: *A glorious heather garden.*

73

Cider Ham Fingers

This is not going to be a recipe exactly,
but rather a method.

Select a couple of ham steaks, as close to 1/2 inch thick as you can get them, and allow 4 to 5 ounces of meat per serving. Trim off all the fat, and if there's a bone, remove that too. Cut the ham into strips 1/2 to 3/4 inch wide. Place the ham strips in a shallow bowl and cover with apple cider. Marinate for several hours. Spread the strips on a baking sheet in a single layer. Run under a preheated broiler and brown slightly, turning once. Serve warm.

ABOVE, FROM LEFT: *A Mendocino garden in full bloom; front stoop detail, a comfortable corner for reading; the pump house.* BELOW, FROM LEFT: *Porthole-framed seascape; painted bedroom armoire; cosmos, petunias, and other blossoms in the garden.*

SATURDAY NIGHT SUPPER

PORK MEDALLIONS WITH PRUNES AND PORT • SIMPLE SAUTEED ASPARAGUS

BUTTERED BULGUR WITH BLACK OLIVES • COCONUT NUTMEG MILK SHERBET

It's funny what will spring the idea for a meal. In this case, we just happened to have a bag of California prunes, which someone had passed along to us, and naturally we thought of using them with pork—hence the main course of pork medallions with prunes and port. There were asparagus in the market so they were added. And I had lately been experimenting with various kinds of grains, and that's how we came to use buttered bulgur wheat.

The ice cream is something I came up with some time ago and so it became the dessert. It was one of those meals that just fell into place.

ABOVE: *Pork Medallions with Prunes and Port, along with the asparagus and bulgur.* OPPOSITE: *Dinner overlooking the cove.*

Pork Medallions
with Prunes and Port

You'll find this elegant little dish fast and easy.

1 1/2 pounds trimmed boneless pork loin

Salt and pepper

Flour

2 tablespoons butter

3/4 cup chicken stock

3/4 cup port

12 pitted prunes, cut in half

Preheat the oven to 200 degrees.

Cut pork into 12 slices. Season with salt and pepper and then dredge in flour, shaking off excess.

Heat butter in a skillet over medium-high heat and brown the pork a minute on each side, turning only once. Remove to a platter and keep warm in the oven.

Deglaze the pan with the chicken stock and port. Add the prunes and increase heat to high. Reduce, stirring, until the sauce coats the back of a spoon, 6 to 8 minutes.

Arrange 3 pork medallions on each plate and spoon some sauce over each. Top with 2 prune halves.

Serves 4

Simple Sautéed Asparagus

Blanch the asparagus just before you start the pork.

36 small to medium asparagus stalks

Salt

1 tablespoon peanut oil

1 tablespoon rice wine vinegar

Break ends of asparagus off by holding the tip in one hand and the stalk end in the other and bending stalk until it breaks. Stalk will break off where the tender part begins. Place the tips in a pot of well-salted boiling water. Blanch for 3 minutes. Drain and pat dry. Cut on the diagonal into 1-inch pieces.

Heat the oil in a large skillet over high heat. Sauté the asparagus, tossing, for 1 1/2 minutes, until just crisp-tender. Off the heat, toss in the vinegar and salt to taste.

Serves 4

Buttered Bulgur
with Black Olives

Many people think of bulgur wheat only as something to use to make tabbouleh. That's too bad—it has a marvelous nutty flavor when served hot. Try this.

2 cups rich chicken stock

1 cup bulgur wheat

1 tablespoon unsalted butter

1/4 cup pitted and coarsely chopped oil-cured black olives

Place the stock in a small saucepan and stir in the bulgur. Cover and bring quickly to a boil. Turn back to simmer and cook, covered, until the wheat is soft and the liquid has been absorbed. Stir in the butter.

To serve, make a mound of bulgur on each plate and sprinkle with the chopped black olives.

Serves 4

Coconut Nutmeg Milk Sherbet

I'm very fond of frozen milks and ices, and this is a particular favorite. You can also make this with low-fat milk.

2 1/2 cups sweetened grated coconut

3 cups milk

1/4 cup tightly packed brown sugar

3/4 to 1 teaspoon grated nutmeg

Salt

Cook the coconut in a heavy saucepan over medium heat, stirring constantly, until it begins to caramelize. Set aside a couple tablespoons to use as topping. Pour in the milk and bring to a simmer. Add the brown sugar. Stir and simmer until sugar is dissolved. Pour into a food processor and process until smooth. Allow to cool, then chill. Stir in nutmeg and a pinch of salt. Freeze in an ice-cream maker, following manufacturer's directions.

Makes about 8 servings

TOP: *Coconut Nutmeg Milk Sherbet.* ABOVE: *Ocean sunset.*

Hearty Lunch

Penne with Cabbage and Lamb

Mixed Green Salad with Mild Cheese

Walnut Tart

In this part of California, by the ocean, the word *breathtaking* always seems to come to mind. It's not only because of the coastline, which seems to change constantly with the light, but also because of the flowers and gardens that overflow with blossoms. The place we were visiting was typical, but if anything more beautiful than most.

When fall comes, I like good flavorful meat sauces on pasta, so here's a sauce using lamb on a bed of lightly steamed cabbage. As you can imagine this is a pretty filling dish. We didn't need anything but a little green salad and cheese to get to us to dessert, which was made with more of those local walnuts and honey.

RIGHT: *The lunch table in the garden.*

Penne with Cabbage and Lamb

The lamb sauce has to cook for three hours, but it's the sort of sauce that can be made a few days in advance—as a matter of fact, it's better if it is. And of course, if you've made the sauce in advance, the meal will be a snap to do.

LAMB SAUCE

1 ounce dried porcini mushrooms

2 cups hot water

10 tablespoons olive oil

8 cups sliced onions

3 1/2 tablespoons minced garlic

1/2 pound fresh white mushrooms, sliced

1 1/2 pounds very well trimmed boneless lamb shoulder or leg, cut into 1-inch pieces

Salt and pepper

Flour, for dredging

1 1/2 cups dry white wine, warmed

2 cups beef stock, warmed

1 large bay leaf

5 4-inch sprigs fresh rosemary

HOT OIL

1 tablespoon red pepper flakes

1/2 cup olive oil

CABBAGE

1 large head green cabbage, about 2 pounds, cored and coarsely shredded

3 tablespoons rice wine vinegar

1 teaspoon salt

1 teaspoon pepper

ASSEMBLY

1 pound penne

Make the lamb sauce. Place the porcini in a bowl and cover with the hot water. Allow to sit for at least 1 hour. Drain, reserving the liquid. Pour liquid through a fine cloth to remove any grit. Set aside.

Heat 4 tablespoons of the oil in a large skillet and sauté the onions until brown, about 12 minutes. Add garlic and sauté another minute. Remove the onions and garlic with a slotted spoon and set aside.

Add 2 more tablespoons of the oil to the pan and sauté the white mushrooms until golden, about 2 minutes. Remove and add to the onions and garlic. Set aside.

Salt and pepper the lamb pieces liberally and dredge them in flour. Using the same pan and the remaining oil, sauté the meat in batches until very brown.

When all the meat is browned, return it to the pan along with the onion mixture and the porcini mushrooms. Add the wine, stock, mushroom liquid, bay leaf, and rosemary. Bring to a boil, reduce to a simmer, cover, and cook very slowly for 2 hours, stirring occasionally. Remove the lid and simmer for another hour or until the meat is falling apart and the sauce is thick. If necessary, thin the sauce with just a little water or stock. Correct seasoning.

Make the hot oil. Combine the pepper flakes and oil in a small saucepan. Heat over medium heat. When oil is hot but not boiling, remove from heat and set aside to cool. Strain before using, discarding pepper flakes.

Make the cabbage. Place the cabbage in a glass bowl and toss in remaining ingredients. Cover tightly with plastic wrap. Make a steam hole in the top and cook in the microwave on highest setting until crisp-tender, about 5 minutes in a full-power oven. Allow to rest, still covered, for another several minutes. If it's not cooked to your taste, you can cook it slightly longer, but it should not be too limp.

To do this without a microwave, combine the cabbage and other ingredients in a stainless-steel skillet. Cook over medium heat, stirring frequently, until it's crisp-tender, about 5 minutes.

Assemble the dish. Cook the pasta according to package directions. Toss with 2 tablespoons of the strained hot oil (reserve any leftover oil for another time) and all the cooked cabbage. Divide among 8 warmed serving bowls and top each with lamb. (Do not serve with cheese.)

Serves 8

ABOVE: *Penne with Cabbage and Lamb.*
OPPOSITE: *Adirondack chair with blooming companion.*

Mixed Green Salad
with Mild Cheese

*We used a mixture of local lettuces and tossed them
with this simple vinaigrette. And since we didn't have cheese
on the pasta, we had wedges of mild cheese here. Any
good chèvre will do, and so will Monterey jack.*

1 tablespoon fresh lemon juice

2 tablespoons rice wine vinegar

2 tablespoons canola oil

7 tablespoons olive oil

Salt and pepper

Whisk all the ingredients together. Taste and correct
the seasoning.

Makes about ¾ cup, enough for 8 servings

Walnut Tart

*You might try this with a mixture
of nuts in place of walnuts by themselves. This
pie is fairly rich, so serve thin slices.*

PASTRY

1 cup all-purpose flour

½ cup chilled unsalted butter, cut into 8 pieces

Pinch of salt

1 tablespoon sugar

3 tablespoons ice water

FILLING

1½ cups sugar

⅓ cup water

Pinch of cream of tartar

1¼ cups heavy cream, heated

4 tablespoons honey

3 cups coarsely chopped walnuts

1½ tablespoons grated orange rind

Whipped cream and grated orange rind, for top (optional)

Make the pastry. Place flour, butter, salt, and sugar in a
food processor and process with a few pulses of the
machine. Sprinkle the water over it all and continue to
process until just before a ball begins to form. Gather into
a ball and flatten between 2 sheets of waxed paper.
Refrigerate for about 20 minutes.

Meanwhile, preheat the oven to 375 degrees.

Place chilled dough on a floured board and roll out.
Line a 9-inch pie pan with it, pricking the bottom with
the tines of a fork. Line with lightly oiled foil, oiled side
down, and place pie weights or dried beans on the foil .
Bake for 15 to 20 minutes or until pastry is set and beginning to brown.

Make the filling. Combine the sugar, water, and cream of
tartar in a heavy pot and cook over medium-high heat,
stirring as the sugar melts. Allow to boil without stirring
until a light caramel color, about 9 minutes. Carefully stir
in the heated cream and cook for another minute or so,
stirring, until well blended. Remove from heat. Stir in the
honey, nuts, and orange rind. Pour into the partially
cooked shell and bake until the filling is set and the crust
is well browned, about 25 to 30 minutes. Cool.

If desired, top with whipped cream and sprinkle with
more grated orange rind.

Serves 10 to 12

A nasturtium border.

TOP: *Mixed Green Salad with Mild Cheese.* ABOVE: *Walnut Tart, topped with whipped cream and orange rind.*

Lenox,
Massachusetts

THE BERKSHIRES BEGIN TO RISE in the top corner of Connecticut and continue to roll through western Massachusetts. There are places close to Lenox where the landscape opens up onto vistas that resemble a more verdant Tuscany, with hills crowned by dense stands of pine, ash, spruce, chestnut, hemlock, oak, maple, and birch. Winter locks these hills in a picture-postcard stillness with snow banked high against jagged rock outcroppings, brilliant white against the evergreens.

As compelling as this winter beauty is, it's the summer I love best. The same must have been true for a small group of extremely well-off Bostonians, New Yorkers, and Philadelphians who, in the 1920s and 1930s, built summer cottages in and around Lenox. These "cottages" had dozens of bedrooms (and probably too few bathrooms), galleries, and garages, as well as buildings to house gardeners, chauffeurs, and other servants. But all was not wining, dining, and croquet. Among the original residents was a renowned conductor who managed to get the Boston Symphony Orchestra to camp out in these parts and perform close to Tanglewood, in Lenox. This

piece of iron whimsy started what has become one of the most concentrated, continuing summer arts festivals in the country, and today Tanglewood is the hub of music activity in the region. Within no more than an hour's drive are the Berkshire Theater Festival (new plays and revivals), Jacob's Pillow (dance—traditional and experimental), The Mount (Shakespearean plays), and the Williamstown Playhouse, which stages mostly revivals with a changing company made up of prominent stage and movie actors, actresses, and craftsmen who converge for the summer. Then there are also newer and smaller groups that offer facilities for artists to experiment.

Obviously you could spend the whole summer here quite contentedly saturated in the arts. But should that not be enough, there's the usual tennis, sailing, riding, golf, hiking, and swimming. Down the road a bit is the carefully maintained Hancock Shaker Village.

I go up to the neighborhood of Lenox for a visit almost every summer. When my friends and I are not sampling the arts, we cook. These meals are typical of what we like to prepare in early summer, when it's warm at noon and cool in the evenings.

PRECEDING PAGES:
Holiday party under the tent.
OPPOSITE: *Reminder of a bygone era.*
BELOW: *Looking downstream.*

SOUTH COUNTY SEAFOOD LUNCH

BAKED CLAMS

LOBSTER SOUP

CHEESE PECAN TWISTS

RASPBERRY TIRAMISU

On our way we took a side trip—a detour, really—to South County, Rhode Island—that stretch of coastline between Narragansett and Watch Hill—for lunch with some friends. It would have been a crime not to have taken advantage of the local bounty, so here's our all-seafood lunch: baked clams and a delicious lobster soup.

ABOVE: *On a sunny screened porch.* OPPOSITE: *A seafood lunch table.*

Baked Clams

The clams here are sort of a clams casino.
I'm sure there are many variations of the old classic.

Coarse salt

Tabasco sauce

36 cherrystone clams, scrubbed, shucked, and left on
the half-shell

6 tablespoons unsalted butter, softened

1/4 cup *each* minced chives, parsley, and green bell pepper

1 tablespoon minced garlic

6 slices bacon, each cut into 6 pieces

12 lemon wedges

Preheat the oven to 450 degrees. Cover the bottom of
a sided baking sheet with coarse salt and put in the oven.

Put a drop of Tabasco on each clam on its half-shell
and slip a teaspoon of butter under each clam. Set aside.

Toss together the chives, parsley, green pepper, and
garlic. Set aside.

Fry bacon squares over low heat until translucent but
not browned, several minutes, and drain on paper towels.

Remove the pan from the oven and arrange the clams
on it. Sprinkle each with the chive mixture and top with
a square of bacon. Bake until the bacon crisps, about 5
minutes.

Serve with lemon wedges.

Serves 6

Lobster Soup

This looks like a long, involved recipe, but in truth
lots of it has to do with making the base for the soup. It's not as
difficult as it seems on first sight.

5 pounds live lobsters

3 tablespoons olive oil

2 cups coarsely chopped onions

1 large carrot, coarsely chopped

2 celery ribs, coarsely chopped

1 large leek, white only, coarsely chopped

2 teaspoons minced fresh ginger

2 large garlic cloves, minced

1/4 cup brandy

Pinch of cayenne pepper

2 bay leaves

2 tablespoons minced fresh parsley

5 pounds ripe tomatoes, peeled, seeded, and
coarsely chopped

3 cups fish stock or bottled clam juice

2 cups chicken stock

1 tablespoon tomato paste

Salt and pepper

2 cups cooked white rice

1 tablespoon sherry (optional)

1 tablespoon unsalted butter

1 large potato, cut into 1/2-inch cubes and boiled

1 large red bell pepper, roasted, peeled, seeded, and
cut into 1/2-inch cubes

Put on a large stock pot of water. When boiling,
plunge lobsters in just long enough to kill them. Remove
and pour out water. While lobsters are cooling, wipe out
pot and add olive oil. Sauté onions, carrot, celery, leek,
ginger, and garlic over medium heat for about 5 minutes.
Meanwhile, remove meat from tails and claws of the lobsters. Set aside. Remove the green mass (tomalley) and
any roe (coral) from the body of the lobsters. Crush all
the shells.

Pour the brandy over the sautéed vegetables. Ignite
and allow to burn off. Add crushed shells and any liquid.
Sauté for about another 10 minutes, until vegetables are
completely wilted. Add cayenne pepper, bay leaves, parsley, and tomatoes. Cover and cook about 10 minutes,
shaking pan occasionally. Add the stocks and tomato
paste. Bring to a boil, turn heat back, and simmer for
about 15 minutes, skimming. Scoop out as many large
shell pieces as you can with a slotted spoon and discard.
Place a colander over a large bowl and pour stock
through, pressing as many solids and as much liquid
through as possible. Discard shells and pulp. Measure
stock and if you have more than 6 cups, reduce to that
amount over high heat. Strain through cheesecloth and
season with salt and pepper.

To serve, heat stock and keep warm. Place 1 cup of the
stock and the 2 cups of cooked rice in a food processor
and process to a smooth puree. Whisk the puree into the
hot stock. Stir in sherry. Melt butter in a small skillet and
sauté lobster meat over medium heat until cooked
through, about 3 minutes. Slice meat and divide among 6
heated bowls. Divide the potato and red pepper as well.
Ladle stock over each.

Serves 6

TOP: *Baked Clams.* ABOVE: *Lobster Soup.*

Cheese Pecan Twists

These are made with frozen puff pastry and couldn't be simpler. Incidentally, if at any point while you are preparing these the pastry should become sticky and difficult to work with, return it to the freezer for 3 or 4 minutes.

1 10 x 15-inch sheet of commercial puff pastry

1/4 cup milk

1 large egg white

1 1/4 cups grated Parmesan cheese

3/4 cup finely ground pecans

Preheat the oven to 400 degrees.

Lay pastry on a flat surface. Beat milk and egg white together and brush pastry liberally with it. Mix cheese and pecans and sprinkle half on top of the pastry. Press down lightly. Turn pastry over and brush with the milk-egg wash and sprinkle with the balance of the cheese mixture. Press down lightly. Using a pizza wheel or a sharp knife, cut pastry crossways into 1 x 10-inch strips. Pick up each strip by one end and, holding it vertically, twist it a few times and place on a parchment-lined baking sheet. Bake for 15 to 20 minutes. Do not let pecans burn. Cool on a rack.

Makes 15 twists

Raspberry Tiramisu

This would be equally good made with other kinds of berries. If you should substitute blackberries, remember they can be rather tart. Sprinkle them with a bit of sugar and let them rest before using them.

SPONGE CAKE

2 large eggs, separated

2 tablespoons warm coffee

1 teaspoon vanilla extract

1 teaspoon fresh lemon juice

1/2 cup sugar

Pinch of salt

1/2 cup sifted self-rising cake flour

ASSEMBLY

1 cup cold espresso

2 1/2 cups fresh raspberries

2 tablespoons water

1 cup sugar

1 pound mascarpone cheese

2 cups heavy cream

2 tablespoons dark rum

1 ounce bittersweet chocolate, grated

BELOW, FROM LEFT: *The rocky South County beachfront; Cheese Pecan Twists; Raspberry Tiramisu.*

Make the cake. Cut a piece of waxed paper and fit it into the bottom of a 2-quart soufflé dish. Do not grease the dish. Preheat the oven to 325 degrees.

Combine egg yolks, coffee, vanilla, and lemon juice. Beat with an electric hand mixer at high speed until thickened, about 2 minutes Add sugar and beat another 30 seconds or so to combine well. Set aside. Beat egg whites until foamy, add salt, and beat until whites form stiff peaks. Fold whites into the yolk mixture. Sift flour, a little at a time, over the batter, folding in after each addition. Pour into dish and bake until a tester comes out clean, about 20 to 25 minutes.

Allow cake to rest in the dish for about 30 minutes. Loosen edges and remove from the dish. Allow to cool completely. Peel off waxed paper and leave uncovered to dry out overnight.

Assemble the dish. Cut cake in half, crossways. Lightly toast the 2 cut sides of the cake under the broiler. Put the bottom slice, toasted side up, back into the dish it was cooked in. Sprinkle with ½ cup of the espresso.

Combine raspberries, water, and ½ cup of sugar in a saucepan. Cook over low heat, stirring, until sugar dissolves, about 4 minutes. Set aside. Place cheese, cream, remaining ½ cup sugar, and rum in a bowl and beat with a hand mixer. Spread half of the mixture over the bottom layer of cake in the dish. Cover this with the berries,

spreading them evenly. Place the top layer of cake, toasted side up, over the berries and sprinkle with the balance of the espresso. Spread the balance of the cheese mixture over this and sprinkle with the grated chocolate. Cover with plastic wrap and refrigerate for at least 1 hour before serving. Remove from the refrigerator about 30 minutes or so before serving. Cut out serving portions and top each with raspberry sauce (recipe follows).

Serves 8 to 12

Raspberry Sauce

2 12-ounce packages frozen raspberries

3 tablespoons water

⅓ cup sugar

2 teaspoons grated lemon rind

Combine berries, water, and sugar and gradually melt together over low heat, stirring occasionally. Bring to a slow simmer and cook for 10 minutes. Strain through a fine sieve and allow to cool. Stir in lemon rind and refrigerate, covered.

Makes about 1¾ cups

EARLY EVENING PICNIC

GRILLED CHICKEN BREASTS WITH DRIED

CRANBERRY RELISH • PITA BREAD

CHOPPED SUMMER SALAD

YELLOW CHERRY TOMATOES

WHITE CHOCOLATE CHOCOLATE BROWNIES

You have the makings of a little outdoor feast here. Take along squares of foil and extra paper napkins to wrap around the pita halves to keep them from leaking after they're stuffed with pieces of chicken and a little of the marinade.

RIGHT: *The outdoor table set with picnic fare.*

Grilled Chicken Breasts with Dried Cranberry Relish

You'll need to make this a couple of days in advance. Be sure this is at room temperature. It shouldn't be served directly from the refrigerator.

$1/3$ cup dried cranberries (see Sources) or golden raisins

$1/4$ cup fresh orange juice

6 tablespoons olive oil

2 to $2\frac{1}{4}$ cups coarsely chopped onions

$3/4$ cup coarsely chopped shallots

1 cup balsamic vinegar

$1/3$ cup pecans or walnuts, toasted and chopped

6 skinned and boned chicken breast halves, about
   $2\frac{1}{4}$ pounds

Vegetable oil

Salt and pepper

Shredded mixed garden greens (optional)

Cover cranberries with orange juice in a small nonreactive saucepan. Warm the mixture over medium heat—do not let it boil—then set it aside for an hour. Meanwhile, combine the olive oil, onions, and shallots in a skillet and cook very slowly until wilted, but not browned, about 8 minutes. Add the vinegar, cranberries, and orange juice. Simmer for 4 minutes. Stir in pecans and set aside to cool.

Brush the chicken breasts lightly with vegetable oil, salt lightly, and pepper well. Grill until just done. This will take only a few minutes on either side, depending on the size of the breasts and how close they are to the heat (you could also do this in the broiler).

Spread half the cranberry mixture over the bottom of a shallow dish. Place the grilled breasts on top in a single layer. Cover with remaining mixture and refrigerate, covered, for 2 or 3 days before serving.

Cut each breast half crosswise, then lengthwise. Stuff into pita halves with some of the relish.

Serves 8

The backyard, with a view of the Berkshires.

Chopped Summer Salad

I like this chopped fairly fine except maybe for the tomatoes, which should be a little coarser. If all you can find is big asparagus, blanch it.

1 cup diced red bell pepper

1 cup seeded and coarsely chopped tomato

1 cup shredded zucchini

1 cup thinly sliced (on the diagonal) tender thin asparagus

2 tablespoons olive oil

2 teaspoons balsamic vinegar

8 dashes Tabasco sauce

Salt and pepper

Toss together pepper, tomato, zucchini, and asparagus. Whisk together the remaining ingredients. Dress just before serving (pour out any liquid that may have accumulated in the bottom of the bowl of vegetables before adding the dressing).

Serves 8

White Chocolate Chocolate Brownies

Now here is a combination you'll like.

1 ½ cups all-purpose flour

½ teaspoon baking powder

¼ teaspoon salt

5 ounces bittersweet chocolate

¼ cup *each* unsalted butter and margarine

3 large eggs

1 ½ cups sugar

1 teaspoon vanilla extract

1 teaspoon espresso powder

6 ounces white chocolate, coarsely chopped

1 ½ cups walnuts, 1 cup medium chopped and ½ cup coarsely chopped

Preheat the oven to 350 degrees. Grease a 9 x 13-inch glass baking pan and line with waxed paper. Grease and flour the paper, shaking out excess flour. Set aside.

Sift the flour, baking powder, and salt onto a plate or sheet of waxed paper and set aside.

Melt the bittersweet chocolate, butter, and margarine together over low heat in a small pot. Stir to mix and allow to cool.

Place the eggs and sugar in a small bowl and mix with a hand mixer at high speed until sugar has dissolved and mixture is light. Beat in the melted chocolate mixture. Stir in the vanilla and espresso powder. Blend in the flour mixture ½ cup at a time. Stir in white chocolate and the cup of medium chopped walnuts.

Scrape the batter into prepared pan and smooth top. Sprinkle the coarsely chopped walnuts on top. Bake 35 minutes. Allow to cool for 8 to 12 minutes, then cut into 24 squares. Cool completely in the pan before inverting onto a serving platter and removing the waxed paper. Separate into squares.

Makes 24

TOP, FROM LEFT: *Arts and Crafts outdoor lantern; front hall finial; stained glass panel.* LEFT: *The stone and shingle house we visited.* ABOVE: *Chopped Summer Salad.*

SUNDAY DINNER

BEST YANKEE MEATLOAF WITH

OVEN-CURED TOMATOES

NEW POTATOES BAKED IN STOCK

GARDEN PEAS IN SHALLOT BUTTER

APRICOT TARTS

It's a pity that more people don't think of meat-loaf as a proper dish to serve guests. Everyone loves it—so why not? Accompaniments here are new potatoes baked in stock and fresh garden peas. For dessert, a puffy little apricot tart.

The meatloaf and potatoes cook about the same length of time and at the same tempera-ture—so do them together.

RIGHT: *Sunday dinner at garden's edge.*

Best Yankee Meatloaf with Oven-Cured Tomatoes

*This meatloaf has a fine texture, and I think it's best
sliced fairly thin. Of course, leftovers are great for sandwiches.
Use a good sandwich loaf for the bread crumbs, don't trim
off the crusts, and don't make the crumbs too fine.
You'll love the tomatoes that top the meatloaf.
Although they aren't complicated to prepare, they do cook
a long time. I usually make them ahead in fairly large
batches because they have many uses. However, if time is short,
make a simple tomato sauce with lots of onions, a little
garlic, a carrot, a sprig of fresh tarragon, and finish it with
a teaspoon or two of wine vinegar to pique its flavor.*

1 pound ground beef

1 pound ground pork

1 pound ground veal

1 1/2 cups chopped shallots

1 1/2 cups chopped celery

1 tablespoon margarine

1 tablespoon vegetable oil

4 large garlic cloves, minced

4 large eggs, lightly beaten

2 tablespoons Worcestershire sauce

2 teaspoons soy sauce

2 tablespoons Dijon mustard

1 tablespoon chili powder

3/4 teaspoon dried thyme

1 teaspoon salt

3/4 teaspoon black pepper

2 cups fresh bread crumbs, dampened slightly with 2
   tablespoons red wine or water

1 pound bacon, blanched 3 minutes

Oven-Cured Tomatoes (recipe follows)

Preheat the oven to 375 degrees.

Combine the 3 meats well with your hands and set
aside. In a medium skillet, sauté the shallots and celery in
the margarine and oil until just beginning to wilt, about 2
to 3 minutes. Add the garlic and cook another minute.
Cool slightly and combine with the meats. Mix the eggs,
Worcestershire, soy sauce, mustard, chili powder, thyme,
salt, and pepper. Pour over meats and mix. Mix in bread
crumbs.

Lay about two-thirds of the bacon across the bottom
of a large, low-sided pan. Pat the meatloaf mixture into
the pan, mounding it slightly in the middle, and bring
side bacon strips up and onto the top, pressing in place.

Use the rest of the bacon to cover the top of the meatloaf. Bake for 1 hour 30 minutes, or until browned.

Allow to rest for 10 minutes before slicing. Top each
serving with an Oven-Cured Tomato.

Serves 8

Oven-Cured Tomatoes

6 fresh medium tomatoes

2 tablespoons olive oil

1 tablespoon minced garlic

1 tablespoon chopped fresh thyme

Salt and pepper

Dip the tomatoes in boiling water for 8 to 10 seconds,
then immediately into ice water. Slip off the skins and cut
out the stem end. Slice the tomatoes in half crosswise.

Line a baking pan with foil and oil it lightly. Place the
tomatoes on the sheet, cut side down. Rub each tomato
half with the oil and then sprinkle with the garlic, thyme,
and salt and pepper.

Place in the oven. Turn oven on to 225 degrees and
bake for 5 to 5 3/4 hours or until tomatoes are soft but still
retain their shape. Cool. Refrigerate, covered with olive
oil, in a tightly closed container. Bring them to room
temperature before serving.

Makes 12 halves

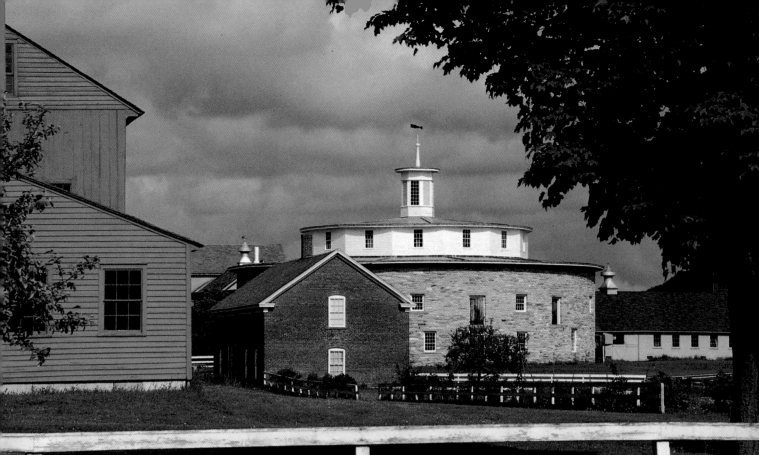

Nearby Hancock Shaker Village. ABOVE: *Looking toward the Round Stone Barn, past the Laundry and Machine Shop (left) and the Poultry House.* BELOW: *The Brick Dwelling, Ministry Wash House, and Sister's Dairy and Weave Shop.* RIGHT: *Entrance to the Sisters' Dairy and Weave Shop, The Privy, and the Round Stone Barn.*

New Potatoes Baked in Stock

Although these potatoes are best served about 10 minutes out of the oven, they can be reheated if necessary. They are even good the next day.

4 tablespoons unsalted butter

3 pounds scrubbed new potatoes, unpeeled, cut into
$\frac{1}{8}$-inch slices, and soaked in cold water for 30 minutes

Salt and pepper

3 large garlic cloves, minced

$\frac{1}{2}$ pound Emmentaler cheese, shredded

1 $\frac{1}{3}$ cups chicken stock, heated

Preheat the oven to 375 degrees. Use 2 tablespoons of the butter to grease a 9 x 13-inch baking dish.

Drain the potatoes and dry them with paper towels. Place one-quarter into the prepared dish. Sprinkle with salt and pepper, a third of the garlic, and a quarter of the cheese. Dot with butter. Make 3 more layers the same way dotting with a little butter as you go along (no garlic goes on top). Pour in the stock. Bake for 1 $\frac{1}{2}$ hours. You can cover it loosely with foil for the last 15 minutes or so if the top is getting too browned. Allow to rest for about 10 minutes before serving.

Serves 8

Garden Peas in Shallot Butter

2 cups water

Salt and pepper

6 cups fresh green peas, about 8 pounds in the pod

$\frac{1}{2}$ cup minced shallots

5 tablespoons unsalted butter, softened

Bring the water to a boil, salt it well, and add the peas. Cook over medium-high heat until tender, about 5 minutes. Cover and allow to rest for 5 minutes. Drain.

While the peas are cooking, sauté the shallots in 1 tablespoon of the butter until wilted, about 5 minutes. Season to taste with salt and a little pepper if desired. Mash the shallots into the balance of the butter.

To serve, toss the hot peas with most of the butter, reserving about 2 tablespoons so you may place a dab on top of each serving.

Serves 8

Apricot Tarts

If you can't find commercial puff pastry, just make an apricot cobbler. I've only made puff pastry from scratch a couple of times, and I'm too lazy to do it for a simple dessert like this. These tarts are best if they are eaten within an hour of their coming come out of the oven.

$\frac{1}{2}$ pound frozen commercial puff pastry (2 sheets)

8 ripe apricots

4 teaspoons fresh lemon juice

2 teaspoons sugar

2 to 3 tablespoons apricot jam, melted

Flavored whipped cream

Allow the pastry to thaw until malleable but still very cold. Dust lightly with flour and roll out each sheet into a 10-inch square. Cut each sheet into four 5-inch squares and place on baking sheets. Chill for 30 minutes.

Preheat the oven to 400 degrees. Dip the apricots briefly into boiling water, then ice water. Peel and stone the apricots, and cut each half into 4 slices. Toss with the lemon juice and sugar. Prick dough with a fork and place the apricot slices in a butterfly pattern on each square. Bake until puffed and golden, about 20 minutes. Allow to cool on a rack and then brush each with melted jam.

Serve with lightly whipped cream flavored with peach or apricot brandy.

Serves 8

Stone foundation detail.

TOP: *An individual Apricot Tart.* ABOVE: *Hancock Shaker Village's Meeting House.*

Round Top, Texas

HECTIC FUN IS NOT what's in store for Houston natives who head to Round Top for a long weekend. Round Top—a village with a population at this writing of 81—beckons precisely because it's *not* like home. But first let's *get* there.

The first part of the journey is spent negotiating miles of freeways through a numbingly familiar jumble of franchised businesses and distant malls. Then we turn off onto what is designated a "farm road," and pastures accented with oaks open out into glorious vistas that in spring are vivid green and spread with an incomparable show of wildflowers. The actual drive from Houston may take only about an hour and a half but in many ways it takes you back in time. Houses are far apart and are most often glimpsed in the distance. Villages with names like New Ulm and Industry look a whole lot like they did fifty years ago. There are still old general stores along the way, selling gas from decrepit pumps out front and a jumble of staples inside. Windmills are still there to raise water.

But Round Top does have other attractions besides timeless tranquillity and quiet beauty. About thirty-five years ago Faith and

Charles Bybee became interested in the history of the Anglo- and German-American colonists who were the first to settle the vast wilderness between the Colorado and Brazos rivers. They eventually created Henkel Square, a mix of restored nineteenth-century buildings that became a "museum village" in Round Top. Others followed. The Reeds began restoring historic buildings in and around Round Top, and the formidable Miss Ima Hogg restored a group of period houses in Winedale, creating another outdoor museum.

So you see it's interest in the region's history that's the heart of Round Top and environs. Because of the area's focus on early art and country furnishings, an antiques fair is held in early April when the wildflowers bloom. It has become one of the largest of its kind in the state. Then about twenty years ago something called Festival Hall was begun, the brainchild of pianist James Dick. Here in summer advanced students and a world-renowned faculty converge to take part in the intense summer music programs. From April to August there are concerts and special programs. So it happened a little sweet music was added to the frontier mix.

PRECEDING PAGES:
Family hat rack.
OPPOSITE: *Road to the farm.*
BELOW: *Looking to the rolling hills of Round Top.*

Texas Quail Dinner

SKILLET-COOKED QUAIL • WHIPPED SWEET POTATOES

GRILLED YELLOW SQUASH AND TOMATO • MONKEY BREAD

TEXAS PECAN CAKE WITH BOURBON CUSTARD SAUCE

One of the great treats about eating in Texas is being lucky enough to know someone who hunts and being able to dine on wild quail. The flavor of wild birds is a dozen times better than the farm-raised variety. To go with the quail are whipped sweet potatoes, grilled yellow squash, and another Texas favorite, monkey bread. Dessert is a tall Texas pecan cake with bourbon custard sauce.

ABOVE LEFT: *Skillet-Cooked Quail and the yellow squash.* RIGHT: *Monkey Bread.* OPPOSITE: *Afternoon rain shower.*

Skillet-Cooked Quail

I've been eating quail all my life and I've decided the more simply they are prepared, the better. This recipe fills that bill.

6 large quail
Tabasco sauce
Salt and pepper
Flour
3 tablespoons unsalted butter
3 tablespoons peanut oil

Have your butcher split the quail and remove the rib cage, breast bone, wings, and wishbone. Flatten each slightly by placing the bird halves between 2 sheets of waxed paper and giving them a few whacks with the side of a cleaver. Put a drop of Tabasco on each side of the quails and rub it in. Sprinkle well with salt and pepper. Dredge in flour, shaking off excess.

Heat 2 very large skillets and divide the butter and oil between each. When bubbly, place quail halves in, skin sides down. Cook for about 3 minutes over low-medium heat. Turn and cook for another 3 minutes. Use a small heavy skillet to weight the quails down and cook an additional 2 minutes. Remove weights and turn, cooking until golden on the other side, about 3 minutes. If quails are not golden by this time, turn up the heat to finish them.

Serves 6

Whipped Sweet Potatoes

Sweet potatoes are another food I love. Here again, the simpler they are the better.

6 medium sweet potatoes, baked until soft
$\frac{1}{2}$ cup unsalted butter
$1\frac{1}{2}$ teaspoons salt
$\frac{3}{4}$ teaspoon black pepper

Peel the potatoes while they're hot. Mix with the butter, salt, and pepper. Use a hand mixer to beat until smooth. May be rewarmed, covered in a low oven.

Serves 6 or more

Table set with the quail dinner.

Grilled Yellow
Squash and Tomato

*Yellow tomatoes are best for this dish, but
use red ones if the yellow tomatoes are not available.*

4 medium garlic cloves, minced

1/2 cup olive oil

1/4 cup balsamic vinegar

Salt and pepper

1 1/2 pounds yellow squash cut into 1/4-inch slices

2 green onions, sliced fine, with some green

1/4 cup minced shallots

1 large yellow tomato, coarsely chopped

Preheat a grill or broiler. Combine garlic, oil, vinegar, salt, pepper, and squash. Marinate for 10 to 15 minutes. Drain the squash, reserving the marinade, and grill until golden. (The timing will depend on how hot the grill is and how far the grate is from the heat.)

Chop the squash into large chunks and place in a bowl. Add the remaining ingredients as well as the marinade. Toss lightly.

Serves 6

Monkey Bread

Texans love this simple bread, and you'll love it too.

1 cup milk

1/2 cup plus 5 tablespoons unsalted butter

1/4 cup sugar

1 teaspoon salt

1 package active dry yeast

3 1/2 cups all-purpose flour

Preheat the oven to 400 degrees.

Place the milk, 1/2 cup butter, sugar, and salt in a small saucepan. Warm over low heat just until the butter melts. Set aside to cool down to about 110 degrees, then stir in the yeast. Put flour in a large bowl and pour in yeast mixture. Stir to combine. Cover with a tea towel and allow to rise until doubled in bulk in a warm, draft-free spot, about an hour and 15 minutes.

Melt the remaining butter. Punch down the dough and roll into golf-ball–size balls. Roll each in the melted but-

ter and place in a 10-inch tube pan. Cover and allow to rise 45 minutes, until doubled in bulk. Bake for 25 minutes, or until golden on top. Allow to cool for about 5 minutes before turning out onto a warmed serving plate.

Serves 8 to 12

Texas Pecan Cake
with Bourbon Custard Sauce

*This cake keeps very well, and it's even better the
second day. I'm giving you a recipe for a cold bourbon-
flavored custard sauce to go with it, but bourbon whipped cream
would be equally good, or just plain vanilla ice cream.*

2 cups all-purpose flour

1/2 teaspoon grated nutmeg

2 pounds pecan halves

1 1/4 cups sugar

1 cup unsalted butter, softened

3 large eggs

1/2 cup bourbon

1/2 teaspoon baking soda

1/2 cup water

Preheat the oven to 300 degrees and grease and flour a 10-inch tube pan.

Combine 1 1/2 cups of the flour with the nutmeg and set aside. Toss the remaining 1/2 cup of flour with the pecans and set aside. Cream the sugar and butter until light, and then beat in eggs one at a time. Beat in the bourbon. Dissolve the baking soda in the water. Mix half the 1 1/2 cups of flour into the batter, then stir in the soda water. Beat in the remaining flour, then fold in the pecans. Spoon batter into prepared pan and rap the pan to get rid of air pockets. Bake until a cake tester comes out clean. Start testing after about an hour and keep a good eye on it. Don't overcook this cake—it'll dry out.

Serve with Bourbon Custard Sauce (see page 121).

Serves 12 or more

TOP: *Conversation on the back gallery.* ABOVE: *Texas Pecan Cake with Bourbon Custard Sauce.*

Bourbon Custard Sauce

1 tablespoon unsalted butter, softened

3 large eggs, beaten

$\frac{1}{2}$ cup plus 2 tablespoons sugar

3 cups low-fat milk

1 $\frac{1}{2}$ teaspoons vanilla extract

Freshly grated nutmeg

1 tablespoon bourbon, more or less

Preheat the oven to 350 degrees and put on a kettle of water to heat.

Butter a 1-quart soufflé dish with the softened butter and set aside.

Whisk together the eggs and sugar. Stir in the milk and vanilla. Pour through a strainer into the prepared dish and sprinkle the top with nutmeg. Bake, in a hot-water bath, until set, about 35 to 40 minutes. Allow to cool, then refrigerate. When ready to serve, pour the bourbon over the custard and whisk it to make a sauce.

Makes about 3 cups

OPPOSITE: *Quilt-covered sofa.* LEFT: *Bedroom desk.* BELOW, FROM LEFT: *Yours truly, hard at rest; mother and daughter; geraniums in the rain.*

OUTDOOR RANCH DINNER

GRILLED VENISON AND WILD BOAR SAUSAGE

WILTED MIXED SUMMER GREENS

HOT SKILLET CORN BREAD

TOMATOES WITH CITRUS DRESSING

FIG PUDDING CAKE

Here is a dinner that should warm any Texan's heart. It's built around grilled sausages with wilted greens, tomatoes, and skillet corn bread. Dessert is a luscious, meltingly smooth custard cake, with a few fig preserves hidden away in the middle. Who could ask for anything more?

RIGHT: *Dinner on the back gallery.*

Grilled Venison
and Wild Boar Sausage

*Venison and wild boar are ranch-raised in Texas, and
are a treat that can be enjoyed year-round. We had an assortment of sausages made from these two as well as a
honey-cured wild boar ham. These come ready to grill or broil,
and you can order them from Broken Arrow Ranch in Ingram,
Texas (see Sources). The recipe below is for venison and wild
boar (pork can be substituted) patties, if you are in the
mood to try your hand at sausage making. Whichever you
choose, serve them with a good mustard and an assortment of
chutneys. The sausage recipe was devised for us by
the people at Broken Arrow Ranch.*

½ cup grated Parmesan cheese

½ cup grated Romano cheese

1 teaspoon cayenne pepper

1 tablespoon minced fresh basil

½ teaspoon grated nutmeg

½ teaspoon ground coriander

2 teaspoons grated orange peel

2 teaspoons grated lemon peel

2 teaspoons salt

4 teaspoons Butter Buds

3 pounds venison, cubed (see Sources)

1 pound wild boar, 50% fat and 50% meat (see Sources)

Combine all ingredients except meat and mix thor-
oughly. Mix the meat and the seasonings together. Chill.
Put through a meat chopper fitted with the coarse plate.
Chill again for a few minutes in the freezer, then mix it
and put it through the chopper a second time. Stuff into
casings or make patties.

Allow to sit a few days in the refrigerator before using
for flavors to meld.

Cook patties, beginning them in a cold skillet, broiler,
or grill.

Serves 6 to 8

Wilted Mixed Summer Greens

*You may use any combination of greens you find
in the market, including mustard greens, turnip greens, beet
greens, collards, chard, spinach, and dandelion.*

4 pounds mixed greens (see Note)

5 tablespoons olive oil

½ cup chicken stock

Salt and pepper

Wash and stem the greens and tear into bite-size
pieces. Heat oil in a very large skillet (these will reduce
considerably, but you will need a large skillet or pot to
start) and add the washed greens. Stir as the greens wilt.
When wilted, add stock, cover tightly, and cook over low
heat until tender, about 15 minutes. Toss in some salt and
a good dose of pepper.

Serves 6

Note: It is rather difficult to give you a precise quantity here, but
it you cook too many, the leftovers freeze. Greens are often sold
in bunches that weigh somewhere between 14 and 18 ounces
each. Then after you strip them of their stems, the weight is usually reduced by half. The weight measure here is with stems.

OPPOSITE: *Venison and wild boar sausage, hot from the grill, with
some wilted greens and a tomato salad.*

Hot Skillet Corn Bread

Corn cut from the cob and a poblano pepper are used in this recipe. Poblanos are not so hot as their fiery cousin, the jalapeños. Canned chili peppers, hot or mild, can be substituted.

You can make this bread two ways, depending on how much crust you like. By reducing the quantity of buttermilk to just enough to hold the batter together—say between $\frac{1}{4}$ and $\frac{1}{2}$ cup—you'll get a rather flat corn bread that is almost all crunch. (You'll have a very stiff batter that you may have to pat into the pan.) That's how we made it for the photograph here.

1 cup yellow cornmeal

1 cup all-purpose flour

1 teaspoon sugar

$1\frac{1}{4}$ teaspoons salt

$3\frac{3}{4}$ teaspoons baking powder

$\frac{1}{4}$ teaspoon baking soda

2 cups corn kernels cut from the cob (or a like amount of frozen kernels, thawed)

$\frac{1}{4}$ cup seeded and minced poblano chili pepper

$1\frac{1}{2}$ cups buttermilk

$\frac{1}{4}$ cup vegetable oil

1 large egg, lightly beaten

Coat a 10-inch cast-iron skillet with vegetable spray. Place it in the oven and preheat oven to 400 degrees.

Sift dry ingredients together into a large bowl. Toss in the corn and pepper. Mix the liquids in another bowl, pour into the dry, and stir. Do not overmix. Quickly remove the hot skillet from the oven and pour the batter in. Bake until golden, about 40 minutes or a little longer if you are making the reduced buttermilk version.

Serves 8 or more

Tomatoes with Citrus Dressing

The slightly sweet taste of this dressing is a very nice complement to the tomatoes.

3 large tomatoes, peeled and thickly sliced

3 tablespoons minced shallots

2 teaspoons grated orange peel

$\frac{1}{2}$ cup fresh orange juice

$\frac{1}{4}$ cup olive oil

3 tablespoons lime juice

1 tablespoon fresh lemon juice

1 teaspoon grated lime peel

1 tablespoon fresh lemon juice

Salt and pepper

Divide tomatoes among 6 plates. Whisk all other ingredients together. Spoon a little of the dressing over each serving of tomatoes.

Serves 6

ABOVE: *Texas girl.*
OPPOSITE: *Crispy corn bread.*
LEFT: *Fence in a field of wildflowers.*
BELOW: *Local hot pepper vinegar.*

Fig Pudding Cake

*Many Texans still make fig preserves. The delicious
little morsels are used in this cake. If you are not lucky enough
to have homemade, use store-bought preserves. Since the
cake should be stale when you assemble this dessert, make it the
day before and leave it out uncovered to dry overnight.*

CAKE

2 large eggs, separated

2 tablespoons warm coffee

1 teaspoon vanilla extract

1 teaspoon fresh lemon juice

$\frac{1}{2}$ cup sugar

Pinch of salt

$\frac{1}{2}$ cup sifted self-rising cake flour

ASSEMBLY

3 large eggs

3 cups milk

$\frac{1}{2}$ cup plus 1 tablespoon sugar

1 teaspoon vanilla extract

Grind of nutmeg

1 cup fig preserves including syrup, chopped and mashed
     lightly together

2 tablespoons softened butter

Make the cake. Cut a piece of waxed paper to fit the bottom of a deep 8-inch soufflé dish and place it in the bottom of the dish. Do not grease the dish. Preheat the oven
to 325 degrees.

Combine the egg yolks, coffee, vanilla, and lemon

juice. Beat with an electric hand mixer at high speed until
thickened, about 2 minutes Add sugar and beat another
30 seconds or so to combine well. Set aside. Beat egg
whites until foamy, add salt, and beat until whites form
stiff peaks. Fold the whites into the yolk mixture. Sift
flour, a little at a time, over the egg mixture, folding in
after each addition. Pour into the prepared pan and bake
until a tester comes out clean, about 25 minutes.

Allow to rest in the pan for about 30 minutes before
loosening the edges and removing from the dish. Allow
to cool completely. Peel off the waxed paper and slice the
layer in half, crosswise. Leave it uncovered to dry out
overnight.

Assemble the dessert. Put a kettle of water on to boil and
preheat the oven to 300 degrees.

Put the eggs in a small pitcher and whisk lightly.
Whisk in the milk, $\frac{1}{2}$ cup sugar, vanilla, and nutmeg. Set
aside. Butter an 8-inch soufflé dish and place the bottom
slice of the cake in it. Spread this with the fig preserves.
Add the top layer of the cake and spread it with the softened butter. Put the dish in a larger ovenproof pan. Pour
the custard through a strainer over the top of the cake,
lightly beating it as you pour. Sprinkle with the remaining tablespoon of sugar. Surround the dish with boiling
water and bake until set, about 1 hour and 15 minutes.
Remove from water bath and allow to cool. Refrigerate,
covered. You may serve this from the soufflé dish or turn
it out onto a serving plate by loosening the edges and
inverting it over the plate and holding the plate in place
while giving it a firm downward shake.

Serves 8 to 10

SUNDAY BREAKFAST

BEEFSTEAK HASH WITH EGGS

CHOPPED AVOCADO, ONION, TOMATO,

AND HOT PEPPER SALAD

QUICK BUTTERMILK ROLLS

ROUND TOP CHOCOLATE CHIP PIE

They like hearty breakfasts in these parts, espe-cially on Sunday. This menu includes a beef-steak hash that has the breakfast eggs cooked right in it. Such a dish fills the "hearty" bill, so accompaniments are a simple salad of avocado and tomatoes, piqued with a bit of onion and the ubiquitous jalapeño and homemade rolls.

Dessert is a local pie. Pretty rich—so just a little slice will suffice.

RIGHT: *A late breakfast set out on a rustic table.*

Beefsteak Hash with Eggs

Don't let the length of the ingredient list put you off. This is no more difficult to prepare than a pot of chili, so forge ahead.

¾ pound slab bacon, cut into ¼-inch dice

1 tablespoon olive oil

4 cups coarsely chopped onions

2½ cups coarsely chopped green bell peppers

1½ pounds coarsely chopped sirloin

2 heaping tablespoons minced garlic

16-ounce can of tomatoes, including juice

1 tablespoon tomato paste

2 teaspoons minced canned jalapeño peppers

2 teaspoons chili powder

2 teaspoons salt

1 teaspoon black pepper

½ cup long-grain rice

1 tablespoon water

¼ cup minced fresh parsley

2 tablespoons butter

2 teaspoons red wine vinegar

2 dashes Tabasco sauce

6 large eggs

Cover bacon with water and bring to a boil. Simmer for 10 minutes. Drain and pat dry.

Preheat the oven to 350 degrees and grease an 8 x 12-inch low-sided baking dish.

Place olive oil in a large skillet and sauté the blanched bacon until golden, 5 to 7 minutes. Remove with a slotted spoon and drain on paper towels. Pour out all but 1 tablespoon of the fat, add onion and green peppers, and cook over medium heat until well wilted, about 10 minutes. Stir in chopped sirloin and garlic. Sauté until meat loses its red color, 5 to 6 minutes. Add reserved bacon and tomatoes, tomato paste, jalapeños, chili powder, salt, pepper, rice, water, and parsley. Mix well and scrape into the prepared pan. Smooth the top and cover tightly with foil. Bake for 30 minutes. Remove from oven and stir so the rice will cook evenly. Smooth and cover again tightly. Cook another 30 minutes.

Meanwhile, brown the butter in a small skillet. Stir in the vinegar and Tabasco, and set aside.

When hash has cooked an hour, remove it from the oven. Use a teacup sprayed on the bottom with vegetable spray to make 6 indentations in the hash. Break an egg into each one. Cover loosely with the foil and return to the oven. Bake for 5 minutes. Remove foil and top each egg with a teaspoon or so of the brown butter mixture. Bake uncovered until eggs are done, 5 minutes or more. Cut into 6 portions, each with an egg in the middle.

Serves 6

Chopped Avocado, Onion, Tomato, and Hot Pepper Salad

Use a Haas avocado for this if possible. Haas is the one with the dark, rough skin.

3 tablespoons fresh lemon juice

6 tablespoons olive oil

Salt and pepper

1 tablespoon minced fresh cilantro

1 cup medium chopped red onion

2 cups peeled, seeded, and coarsely chopped fresh tomatoes

1 large avocado, peeled, seeded, and coarsely chopped

1 teaspoon minced jalapeño pepper, or to taste

Whisk together the lemon juice, olive oil, salt, pepper, and cilantro. Set aside.

Combine the other ingredients and toss with the vinaigrette.

This can sometimes be rather liquid, so serve it with a slotted spoon.

Serves 6

TOP: *Beefsteak Hash with Eggs, and bowls of the chopped salad.* ABOVE: *Texas ancestor under a blanket of bluebonnets.*

Quick Buttermilk Rolls

*This recipe came to me from my friend Ann Criswell
of The Houston Chronicle.*

1 package active dry yeast

2 tablespoons warm water

¾ cup buttermilk, heated to lukewarm

2 tablespoons sugar

¼ cup melted shortening or vegetable oil

½ teaspoon salt

2¼ cups all-purpose flour

¼ teaspoon baking soda

2 tablespoons unsalted butter

Combine yeast and water and set aside to proof. Mix the warmed buttermilk, sugar, shortening, and salt. Sift flour with the baking soda into a large bowl. Stir yeast into the buttermilk mixture and pour onto the flour. Stir to mix well and allow to rest 10 minutes covered with a tea towel. Roll out to ½ inch thick and form into desired shapes.

Preheat the oven to 425 degrees. Melt butter in a baking pan and place rolls in, turning to coat the tops. Allow to rise 30 minutes.

Bake until golden, about 10 to 12 minutes.

Makes about 2 dozen

ABOVE: *Wildflowers.*
OPPOSITE: *Round Top Chocolate Chip Pie.*

Round Top Chocolate Chip Pie

*This recipe comes from Bud Royer, pie maker
extraordinaire and owner of the Round Top Cafe. It's pretty rich
and sweet, the way folks like desserts in this part of the
country. You could accompany it with ice cream—if you dare.
The crust recipe gives you a generous amount of dough
to work with. Any leftovers can be rolled out, cut into strips,
brushed with egg white, sprinkled with sugar, and baked.
These are good with ice tea, ice cream, or lemonade.*

PASTRY

2 cups all-purpose flour

2 tablespoons granulated sugar (optional)

¼ teaspoon salt

½ cup unsalted butter, chilled and cut into bits

1 large egg yolk

2 to 3 tablespoons ice water

FILLING

1 cup granulated sugar

1 cup brown sugar, tightly packed

1 cup all-purpose flour

2 large eggs, lightly beaten

½ cup unsalted butter, melted

½ cup coarsely chopped toasted pecans or walnuts

½ cup chocolate chips

Make the pastry. Place flour, sugar, and salt in the bowl of a food processor fitted with a plastic blade. Add the butter and the egg yolk. Pulse until mixture resembles coarse meal.

With the motor on, add 2 tablespoons of the ice water and process just until dough masses into a ball (add another tablespoon of water if needed). Remove dough from processor and knead in any remaining flour. Chill, wrapped in plastic, for 30 minutes or so.

Roll out dough and line a deep 10-inch pie pan and set aside. Preheat the oven to 300 degrees.

Make the filling. Mix sugars and flour together. Stir in the eggs and then the butter, combining well. Fold in the nuts and chips. Spread in the prepared crust and bake until a knife inserted in the center comes out clean, 60 to 70 minutes.

Serves 12

Dorset, Vermont

OR MANY PEOPLE VERMONT calls up images of ski trails and firesides, of locked-in white beauty when snow has covered the landscape, of bracing clear air and a muffled stillness that spreads over it all. But to me seeing the place only as a winter hideaway is to miss half its appeal. For in spring and summer this same landscape is swept with voluptuous shades of green as far as you can see in every direction. It's an irresistible time of the year to be in Vermont—particularly in Dorset.

The first hearty settler family stopped here to put down roots around 1769. By 1777 there were probably fifteen families that called Dorset home. A mint was opened in the town with a grant to make copper coins, but when Vermont joined the Union in 1791 as the fourteenth state the mint was out of business.

Dorset prospered in the manner of many of its neighboring communities, with local residents making a comfortable but hard-won living in the Green Mountains from farming, dairying, and trade.

However, it was probably the quarrying, in the middle of the nineteenth century, of the great marble mountain north of the village that was responsible for the town's biggest population explosion, to about 2,000 people.

Nowadays, many of the farmers have abandoned their farms and dairies and have departed for good, but these industries have been replaced by craftsmen and artists—among others—who find the bucolic serenity of the area an inspiration. There is a marvelous inn on the village green, a place that sells quilts down the road, a historical society, a library, and even a summer theater. But I think the clincher is all that natural splendor. It's no wonder to me that Dorset has attracted its share of "summer people" who often are seduced into arriving earlier, and leaving later, each year—some even deciding to put down roots as the first settlers did in 1769. Things have come full circle in a way; only the cast of characters has changed.

PRECEDING PAGES: *At the foot of the Green Mountains; spring spruce-up.* BELOW, FROM LEFT: *Side porch; living room with a collection of finials; rockers at the local inn.*

BUFFET DINNER

BEST BEEF STEW • MASHED POTATOES

AND CAULIFLOWER • SUNFLOWER BREAD

MARINATED CUCUMBERS AND YELLOW

PEPPERS WITH DILL AND MINT

CREAM CHEESE BUNDT CAKE

Here's our party menu. The main dish, a tasty beef stew, can be made the day before, as can the bread and dessert, so all you'll need do on the day of the party is make the salad (in the afternoon) and do the potatoes and cauliflower—which can be finished just before the guests arrive. The stew and potatoes can reheat together.

RIGHT: *The buffet dinner.*

Best Beef Stew

This really should be made the day before. That way it will be easy to degrease. Besides, the flavor will be much enhanced.

4 pounds boneless sirloin, cut into 1 x 2-inch chunks

2 cups hearty red wine

1/2 pound unsmoked slab bacon, cut into 1/4-inch dice

2 tablespoons olive oil

2 large onions, thinly sliced

2 small carrots, scraped and thinly sliced

1/4 cup unsalted butter

1/4 cup all-purpose flour

3 cups chicken or veal stock, heated

2 large garlic cloves, thinly sliced

2 teaspoons tomato paste

1 1/2 teaspoons salt

1/2 teaspoon black pepper

Place the beef in a crockery bowl, add the wine, cover, and marinate, refrigerated, for 3 hours.

Preheat the oven to 325 degrees.

Cover bacon pieces with water, bring to a boil, and simmer for 10 minutes. Drain and dry.

Place olive oil in a Dutch oven and add bacon. Sauté until golden. Remove with a slotted spoon.

Drain the sirloin, reserving the marinade. Dry the meat well and brown it in batches over high heat. Set aside.

Add the onions and carrots to the Dutch oven and sauté until wilted and beginning to brown, about 7 minutes. Remove with a slotted spoon.

Pour out any oil that may be in the Dutch oven. Melt butter over medium heat in the Dutch oven and stir in flour. Cook, scraping the bottom of the pan, until the roux turns a dark golden brown. Stir in the hot stock. This will foam up, so stand back. Simmer a minute or two, then stir in the garlic, tomato paste, and salt and pepper. Add the sautéed vegetables, meat, bacon, and reserved marinade. Bring to a boil quickly on top of the stove. Cover and bake until tender, about 2 hours. Allow to cool, then refrigerate overnight.

Remove the stew from the refrigerator an hour before reheating. Lift off the congealed fat and discard. Reheat in a preheated 325 degree oven until bubbly, about 45 minutes.

If the sauce has reduced and is a bit too thick, thin it out with an extra cup of hot chicken stock.

Serves 8

Mashed Potatoes and Cauliflower

Of course, you can boil the potatoes for this, but I bake them, which I like better. I save the skins (sliced into strips), and at a later date butter and salt them and toast them for hors d'oeuvre.

2 generous cups cauliflower florets and tender stems

Low-fat milk

3 pounds russet potatoes, rubbed with oil and baked

1 large head roasted garlic (see Note)

6 tablespoons unsalted butter

Salt and pepper

Cover the cauliflower with milk in a large saucepan. Bring to a boil, being careful not to let it cook over (that's why you use a large saucepan for this). Turn back to slow boil and cook until just tender, about 10 minutes.

Scoop out the hot potato flesh into a large warm bowl. Squeeze the soft garlic pulp into the potatoes, using as much or as little as you like. Cut butter into pieces and mash in with a hand masher (do not use an electric mixer, as it will make the mixture glutinous). Drain the cauliflower, reserving milk. Mash in with the potatoes, adding about 3/4 cup of the cauliflower milk. Add a little more milk if you would like the potatoes creamier. Salt and pepper to taste.

Butter a casserole and scrape the mixture in. Smooth the top and rub with a bit of butter to make a thin film on top. Set aside, covered with a tea towel, until ready to reheat. (This may be done an hour before dinner.)

To reheat, put into a preheated 325 degree oven, uncovered, for 20 minutes.

Serves 8

Note: To roast garlic, cut a slice off the head to expose the cloves. Rub the cut end with a teaspoon of olive oil, wrap the head with foil, and bake it with the potatoes.

CLOCKWISE FROM TOP: *Best Beef Stew; Dorset city limits; Mashed Potatoes and Cauliflower.*

Sunflower Bread

The recipe for this nutty-tasting bread came from my cohort Lee Klein. Obviously, a good, hearty store-bought loaf could be substituted for this bread—as good as it is.

¹/₂ cup cracked wheat or bulgur

¹/₂ cup rolled oats

¹/₄ cup light brown sugar, tightly packed

2 teaspoons salt

2 tablespoons solid vegetable shortening

³/₄ cup boiling water

2 envelopes active dry yeast

1 cup warm milk (100 to 115 degrees)

2 tablespoons sesame seeds, toasted

2 tablespoons poppy seeds, toasted

1 cup raw sunflower seeds, toasted

¹/₄ cup instant polenta or yellow cornmeal

1 cup whole wheat flour

1¹/₂ cups all-purpose flour

Put the cracked wheat, oats, brown sugar, salt, and shortening in a large mixing bowl. Pour the hot water over this and stir to melt the shortening. Set aside. Sprinkle yeast over the warm milk in a small bowl and set aside for a few minutes to proof. Add the yeast to the cracked wheat mixture and stir in the seeds and polenta. Mix well. Add whole wheat flour and mix well. Add 1¹/₄ cups of all-purpose flour and mix until incorporated. The dough will still be a bit sticky. Sprinkle some of the extra flour on a board and turn the dough out onto it. Knead, gradually incorporating remaining flour, until dough is elastic, about 10 to 15 minutes. Gather into a ball and put in an oiled bowl. Cover and let rise in a warm, draft-free spot until doubled in bulk, about 45 minutes.

Preheat the oven to 350 degrees. Punch down dough. Turn out onto a board and roll into a rectangle about 7 x 12 inches. Starting at the narrow end, roll the dough. Fit it into an oiled 9 x 5 x 3-inch bread pan. Cover and let rise again until dough is above sides of the pan, about 20 minutes. Bake for about 1 hour. Loaf will be light golden and will sound hollow when rapped with your knuckle. Turn it out of the pan immediately and cool on a rack.

Serves 12 or more

Marinated Cucumbers and Yellow Peppers with Dill and Mint

You could serve this as an accompaniment to grilled fish too—a perfect combination.

8 cups thinly sliced peeled cucumbers

4 cups thinly sliced yellow bell peppers

¹/₂ teaspoon minced fresh jalapeño pepper

¹/₄ cup snipped fresh dill

2 tablespoons fresh mint, cut into strips

4 teaspoons salt

¹/₄ cup finely chopped red onion

¹/₄ cup olive oil

4 teaspoons red wine vinegar

¹/₂ teaspoon black pepper

¹/₂ cup coarsely snipped radish sprouts (optional)

Toss the cucumbers, peppers, jalapeño, dill, and mint together with the salt in a shallow bowl. Cover with a plate that fits inside and weight down with a couple of heavy cans. Refrigerate for at least 1 hour. Remove from the refrigerator and drain well, squeezing the vegetables out with your hands. Toss the mixture with the onion, olive oil, vinegar, and pepper. Add sprouts and toss lightly. Salt if necessary.

Serves 8

Honeysuckle.

TOP: *Grazing sheep.* ABOVE: *Sunflower bread.*

Cream Cheese Bundt Cake

Don't let the simplicity of this recipe deceive you; it has a distinctive flavor and texture. And thanks to Mickey Ellis for giving me the recipe for the cake.

¾ cup margarine

6 tablespoons butter

2 cups granulated sugar

6 ounces cream cheese, softened

1½ teaspoons vanilla extract

4 large eggs

2 cups all-purpose flour

Pinch of salt

Blueberry Cinnamon Syrup (optional; recipe follows)

Confectioners' sugar (optional)

Grease and flour a Bundt pan. Cream together the margarine, butter, and sugar until light. Beat in the cream cheese until smooth. Beat in vanilla. Beat in eggs, one at a time, then stir in the flour and salt. Spoon into pan and put in a cold oven. Turn oven on to 275 degrees and bake until tester comes out clean, about 1 hour and 10 minutes (check for doneness after 1 hour).

Allow to cool and remove from pan. Serve with Blueberry Cinnamon Syrup or dust with confectioners' sugar.

Serves 8 or more

OPPOSITE TOP: *Winnowed field.*
ABOVE: *Cream Cheese Bundt Cake with blueberry syrup.*
FAR LEFT: *Red barn against the mountain.* LEFT: *Steeples in nearby Newfane.*

Blueberry Cinnamon Syrup

Here's a case where frozen berries work just fine. And if you do use frozen blueberries, don't cook them; instead, remove hot syrup from the heat and just dump them in.

1 cup sugar

1 cup water

1 long stick of cinnamon, broken in half

2 long strips of lemon peel

10 black peppercorns

1 pint blueberries, picked over

Combine sugar, water, cinnamon, lemon peel, and peppercorns in a saucepan. Stir and bring to a boil, stirring. Add blueberries and cook for a minute or two. Cool, then refrigerate until well chilled.

Makes about 3 cups

SATURDAY NIGHT DINNER

UNCOOKED TOMATO SOUP

GRILLED VEAL CHOPS

EGGPLANT, ZUCCHINI, AND PARMESAN TORTINO

ORANGE, COCONUT, AND DATE AMBROSIA

Now, here's the menu for our big Saturday night dinner. It started with an uncooked tomato soup, followed by grilled veal chops lightly brushed with olive oil and a savory vegetable tortino. We finished off with a refreshing ambrosia.

ABOVE: *Commemorative plaque.* OPPOSITE: *Table by the staircase.*

TOP: *Eggplant, Zucchini, and Parmesan Tortino.* ABOVE: *Uncooked Tomato Soup.* OPPOSITE: *Conversation with the dogs.*

Uncooked Tomato Soup

*You could stir a bit of crab meat or boiled small shrimp
into this soup and make a meal of it.*

3 pounds ripe tomatoes, peeled and seeded

1 medium green bell pepper, seeded and coarsely chopped

1 small cucumber, peeled, seeded, and coarsely chopped

3 large celery ribs, peeled

10 small basil leaves, coarsely chopped

1 tablespoon chopped fresh tarragon

2 tablespoons olive oil

$\frac{1}{4}$ cup tarragon vinegar

Salt and pepper

1 cup vegetable stock

3 tablespoons minced roasted red pepper (optional)

Yogurt or crème fraîche (optional)

Put all the vegetables, herbs, oil, and vinegar in the bowl of a food processor and pulse until roughly chopped. Pour into a large bowl and stir in salt and pepper to taste and stock. If the soup is too thick, thin with a little extra stock. May be garnished with minced roasted red pepper, a dollop of yogurt or crème fraîche, and a sprig of herb. Serve either at room temperature or slightly chilled.

Serves 8 or more

Grilled Veal Chops

*This simple method is just
about the best way to cook a veal chop.*

6 rib veal chops, about 1-inch thick, trimmed

Olive oil

Balsamic vinegar

Salt and pepper

6 lemon wedges

Rub the chops with olive oil, vinegar, salt, and a liberal amount of pepper. Place on the grill or under a preheated broiler. Broil about 5 minutes per side until just slightly pink inside.

Serve with a little extra olive oil and balsamic vinegar drizzled on top. Garnish with a wedge of lemon.

Serves 6

Eggplant, Zucchini, and Parmesan Tortino

The recipe for this tortino, as well as the method for preparing the chops, came courtesy of Michael Romano, chef at Danny Meyer's marvelous New York City restaurant, Union Square Cafe. It's delightful (both the restaurant and the dish).

¾ cup plus 2 tablespoons olive oil

1 pound Spanish onions, peeled and cut into ¼-inch slices

Salt and pepper

1 pound eggplant, peeled and quartered lengthwise, then cut into ¼-inch slices

½ pound zucchini, washed and sliced into ¼-inch rounds

½ pound yellow summer squash, washed and sliced into ¼-inch rounds

5 large eggs

2 tablespoons balsamic vinegar

1 cup heavy cream

½ cup grated Parmesan cheese

Preheat the oven to 325 degrees.

Heat ¼ cup of the olive oil in a large skillet and cook the onions over medium-high heat until very tender, 5 to 6 minutes. Season with salt and pepper and put into a large mixing bowl.

Using another ¼ cup of the olive oil, sauté the eggplant, zucchini, and yellow squash over high heat until tender, 6 to 8 minutes. Add to the onions.

In a medium bowl, whisk together the eggs, ¼ cup of olive oil, the vinegar, cream, and half the Parmesan. Pour this over the vegetables and mix gently.

Use the remaining 2 tablespoons olive oil to oil a 2-inch-deep 2-quart baking dish. Pour in the vegetable mixture. Cover with foil and bake for 45 minutes. Remove foil and sprinkle with the remaining Parmesan. Bake for an additional 15 minutes. Run under the broiler briefly to brown lightly. Allow to rest half an hour, then slice into squares to serve.

Incidentally, this may be made the day before and reheated. With a light tomato sauce, it makes a delicious main course.

Serves 6

Note: As tasty as it is, this has a lot in the way of eggs, oil, and cream. So with Michael's blessing we made a version using slightly less oil and egg substitute for 3 of the 5 eggs and evaporated skim milk for the cream. We made the two dishes at the same time so we could taste them together. I was amazed and pleased to find that the second version tasted almost exactly like the original—only slightly lighter.

Orange, Coconut, and Date Ambrosia

Banana or fresh pineapple or both could be added to this.

5 navel oranges, peeled

1 cup freshly grated coconut

5 large medjhool dates, cut into quarters

2 tablespoons sugar

1 cup fresh orange juice

Dip peeled oranges into boiling water for 20 seconds. This will make it easier to scrape off the remaining pith after oranges are peeled. Cut each orange crosswise into 6 slices. Cut each slice into quarters. Place in a glass bowl. Add coconut, dates, and sugar. Pour orange juice over all and toss. Refrigerate until ready to serve.

Serves 6

ABOVE: *Spring flowers from the garden.*
OPPOSITE: *Stand of silver birch.*

Pass Christian,

Mississippi

ABOUT SEVEN MILES OR so from New Orleans, located on that little toe of Mississippi that is their only Gulf coastline, is a place called Pass Christian. "The Pass," as locals call it, has been a favorite summering destination for generations of New Orleanians. I had a friend, herself a fourth-generation New Orleanian, tell me, "You know, people here think that if they've lived right, when they die they go to the Pass." A visit there will tell you why.

A few blinks and you'll have missed the Pass. If you didn't know they were there, you might not be on the lookout for the fine old houses with wide porches perched on a gentle rise, almost hidden by trees with their shielding old limbs reaching for the ground as well as heaven. Settlements like Pass Christian fascinate me. I'm sure there must be scores like them sprinkled all over the country. Places beloved by people who grew up with them, where grand old houses were built when the building was easy. Quiet and breezy spots for families to escape to in the summer, but often unknown to the rest of the world. You won't find the social competition of the Hamptons here, or the jazz of Aspen, or the shopping streets of Palm Beach. People come to do nothing, but to do nothing in style.

Here are two meals we prepared to make doing nothing even more of a pleasure. Since the porches of Pass Christian are so varied we decided to photograph each meal on a different one.

PRECEDING PAGES: *Fence with roses.* BELOW, FROM LEFT: *Fishing boats; a pier at dawn; tunnel of trees leading to the Gulf.* OVERLEAF: *Porches of the Pass.*

SEAFOOD SUPPER

GULF SHRIMP, CRAB, AND OYSTER STEW

HARD-COOKED EGG AND GARDEN GREEN SALAD • FRENCH BREAD

BROWN SUGAR CUSTARD

I suspect it would be a safe guess that almost every place on a large body of water has some sort of bouillabaisselike dish as part of its cooking repertoire, and it was certainly bound to happen in a locality so near to New Orleans, with all those Frenchmen around. Dishes such as this are much like gumbo in that almost anything goes. So if you get in the mood to try it, feel free to add or subtract according to what you like and what's available when you get around to it.

Actually, this stew is a meal in itself so we didn't have anything but French bread with it, and wine of course, followed by a little salad. Dessert was brown sugar custard with a surprise in the bottom and a fresh strawberry on top. Simple but satisfying, just the way I like it.

ABOVE: *A dish of seafood stew.* OPPOSITE: *Quiet afternoon in the shade.*

Gulf Shrimp, Crab, and Oyster Stew

Many people make the fish base for this dish in large quantities and freeze it in batches large enough to prepare dinner for six or eight.

FISH BASE

1 $\frac{1}{4}$ pounds onions, coarsely chopped

$\frac{1}{4}$ cup olive oil

$\frac{1}{4}$ pound garlic, peeled, cloves left whole

3 pounds fresh tomatoes, seeded and chopped

1 $\frac{1}{2}$ teaspoons dried thyme

1 $\frac{1}{2}$ teaspoons dried oregano

1 tablespoon dried basil

2 bay leaves, crumbled

Pinch of saffron

4 cups fish stock, oyster water, or bottled clam juice

2 $\frac{1}{2}$ teaspoons salt

ASSEMBLY

3 tablespoons olive oil

1 tablespoon minced garlic

1 pound peeled and deveined raw shrimp

1 pound shucked oysters

1 pound crab meat, picked over

1 leek, white part only, cut into thin julienne (optional)

1 small carrot, cut into thin julienne (optional)

$\frac{1}{2}$ red bell pepper, cut into thin julienne (optional)

$\frac{1}{2}$ yellow bell pepper, cut into thin julienne (optional)

Peel of 1 lemon in long strips (optional)

Make the fish base. In a large skillet, sauté the onions in the olive oil until quite soft, about 8 to 10 minutes. Add all other ingredients except stock and salt. Cover, bring to a simmer, and cook 20 minutes. Add stock and bring to a boil, turn back heat, and simmer another 20 to 30 minutes.

Puree the mixture, then strain it, pressing out as much liquid as possible. Add salt.

Complete the stew. Heat 2 tablespoons of the oil in a deep saucepan and cook garlic over medium heat until wilted and beginning to brown, about 4 minutes. Add shrimp. Cook for 1 minute and add the fish base. Simmer 3 to 4 minutes. Add oysters and crab meat. Cook for another 1 to 2 minutes until oysters begin to curl. This makes a very thick stew, which could be thinned out with more liquid (water or fish stock) if desired.

Meanwhile, heat the remaining tablespoon of oil in a small skillet and sauté the julienned garnish vegetables until barely wilted, about 3 minutes.

Serve stew in large bowls garnished with the julienned vegetables and the lemon zest.

Serves 6

Hard-Cooked Egg and Garden Green Salad

Versions of this simple salad have been a Gulf Coast favorite for generations. This makes more vinaigrette than you'll need, but you'll use it later.

VINAIGRETTE

$\frac{1}{4}$ cup red wine vinegar

$\frac{1}{4}$ teaspoon salt

$\frac{1}{2}$ teaspoon pepper

$\frac{1}{2}$ teaspoon Tabasco sauce

1 teaspoon Worcestershire sauce

$\frac{1}{2}$ teaspoon dried marjoram

1 tablespoon honey

1 cup oil

ASSEMBLY

6 cups well-washed mixed garden greens, torn into bite-size pieces

6 hard-cooked eggs, sliced

Salt and pepper

Make the vinaigrette. Whisk or shake all ingredients together until well blended.

Assemble. Divide the greens among 6 salad plates. Top each with slices of egg and some of the vinaigrette. Sprinkle with salt and a good grind of black pepper.

Serves 6

TOP: *The porch, facing the Gulf.* ABOVE: *The table set for supper.*

Brown Sugar Custard

*Custards with a little surprise at the bottom remind
me of my childhood. My grandmother used to use her delicious
homemade strawberry preserves as we've done here, but
you could substitute any fruit preserve or jelly.*

2 cups low-fat milk

1/3 cup granulated brown sugar

Pinch of salt

3 large eggs

1 teaspoon vanilla extract

1/4 to 1/2 cup strawberry preserves

Nutmeg

Fresh strawberries, for garnish (optional)

Preheat the oven to 325 degrees. Generously butter six
1/2-cup ramekins and place in an 8 x 12-inch baking dish.
Put a kettle of water on to boil.

Scald the milk in a medium saucepan. Turn heat back
to very low and stir in brown sugar and salt until dissolved.

Beat the eggs in a bowl and stir in several tablespoons
of the hot milk to heat them. Pour heated eggs into milk,
stirring, and cook for about 1 minute. Remove from heat
and stir in the vanilla.

Divide preserves equally among the ramekins and pour
the custard into them through a sieve. Grate a bit of nutmeg over each. Pour hot water around ramekins and bake
until set, about 35 to 40 minutes. Allow to cool and
refrigerate, covered.

These may be served in the ramekins or turned out
onto individual dessert plates. To remove from the
ramekins, loosen edges with a knife and, holding the
plate securely over the top of the ramekin, invert and give
a downward thrust. Garnish each with a strawberry.

Serves 6

ABOVE RIGHT: *Porch column detail.* RIGHT: *Brown Sugar
Custard.* OPPOSITE: *Entrance to the house.*

COMPANY DINNER

BUTTERMILK CHICKEN WITH

DEEP GRAVY

BUTTERMILK BISCUITS

FRESH BLACK-EYED PEAS

CREOLE TOMATOES WITH

AVOCADO MAYONNAISE

CARAMELIZED SUGAR CAKE

I think, especially in the South, company dinners are always expected to be a bit richer that your daily fare. The menu here, which is a bit of a throwback, fills the bill. And so since we had the buttermilk we made biscuits, which are traditional with such a meal. To round it out there are fresh black-eyed peas and Creole tomatoes. The dessert, a caramel cake, is another old standby.

RIGHT: *Dinner on the screened porch.*

PASS CHRISTIAN

Buttermilk Chicken with Deep Gravy

In the South when they say something is served with deep gravy, they mean with lots of gravy so you can have some to put on your biscuits if you like.

6 large chicken thighs

1 large chicken breast, cut into 4 pieces

1 quart buttermilk

1¾ cups all-purpose flour

Salt

1½ teaspoons paprika

1½ teaspoons pepper

Canola oil, for frying

1½ cups minced onions

1 cup minced green bell pepper

¾ cup minced celery

4 cups chicken stock, heated

Preheat the oven to 375 degrees.

Place chicken pieces in a bowl and cover with buttermilk. Soak for about 1 hour. In the meantime, mix 1½ cups flour, 1½ teaspoons salt, paprika, and 1 teaspoon of the pepper. Drain chicken but do not wipe. Dredge well in the seasoned flour and set on a plate. Over high heat, warm about 1 inch of oil in a large skillet. Quickly brown chicken on both sides, about 1 minute. Place chicken pieces in a single layer in an ovenproof pan. Set aside.

Meanwhile, in another medium skillet combine remaining flour and oil. Make a dark roux over medium-high heat, stirring constantly with a spatula or pancake turner, about 10 minutes. When the roux is dark, add onions and brown lightly, about 4 to 5 minutes. Add green pepper and celery and cook long enough to wilt slightly, a minute or so, stirring constantly. Remove from the heat. Carefully pour out all oil from the skillet in which you browned the chicken but retain any browned bits of flour. Scrape the roux and vegetables into this skillet and stir in the heated stock. Also rinse out the roux skillet with a little of the stock and pour it in with the other mixture. Add remaining pepper and salt to taste. Simmer to thicken. Pour around the chicken and bake, lightly covered, 30 minutes, or until chicken is done.

Serves 6 to 8

Buttermilk Biscuits

A Texas friend, David Tiller, passed this recipe on to me; it was his mother's. The baking method—in a preheated dish— gives them a wonderfully crisp crust, perfect with the gravy.

2 cups all-purpose flour

1 tablespoon baking powder

1 teaspoon salt

½ teaspoon baking soda

½ cup shortening (butter, margarine, or a combination)

1 cup buttermilk

Preheat the oven to 450 degrees. Coat 2 glass baking dishes with vegetable spray and put them in to heat.

Combine the dry ingredients in a large bowl. Cut in the shortening with a pastry blender or 2 knives. Mix in buttermilk. Place on a floured surface and pat down to ½ inch thick. Cut into about 12 biscuits, gathering up the scraps and patting them down again to make the final cuts. Remove heated dishes from the oven. Put biscuits in, touching one another, and bake until golden, about 12 to 14 minutes.

Makes 12

Fresh Black-Eyed Peas

Unless you live in the South, you probably won't be able to find fresh black-eyed peas. If that's the case, use frozen ones.

4 slices thick bacon

¼ cup minced onion

1½ cups chicken stock

Salt and pepper

1 pound shelled black-eyed peas

Fry bacon until brown in a deep pot and drain on paper towels. Pour out all the fat except 1 tablespoon and sauté onion until beginning to brown, about 5 minutes. Pour in stock and bring to a boil. Meanwhile, chop the bacon and add to the stock along with some salt and pepper. When boiling, add peas. Simmer, covered, skimming occasionally, for 25 minutes, until beans are tender.

Serves 6

TOP: *Ancient tree shading the house.* ABOVE: *Wonderfully crisp Buttermilk Biscuits.*

169

Creole Tomatoes
with Avocado Mayonnaise

Everyone in this part of the world looks forward to the arrival of the first Creole tomatoes of the season. Naturally, locals think they're the best, and I'm inclined to agree. But I was born in these parts. Must be in the genes.

6 medium Creole tomatoes, peeled and sliced

Salt and pepper

1 ripe Haas avocado, peeled and seeded

2 tablespoons fresh lime juice

1/4 cup mayonnaise

2 dashes Worcestershire sauce

2 dashes Tabasco sauce

Arrange tomatoes on individual plates and sprinkle with salt and pepper.

Mash the other ingredients together. The amounts are at best mere guidelines. Add more of anything you like.

Serve avocado mayonnaise on the side.

Serves 6

Caramelized Sugar Cake

Aunt Cora, who was the cake maker in our family, used to make this cake. I still love it.

1 1/2 cups granulated sugar

3/4 cup boiling water

2 1/2 cups all-purpose flour

1 1/2 cups pecans, toasted and coarsely chopped

1 teaspoon baking powder

3/4 teaspoon baking soda

3/4 cup butter

2 large eggs, separated

1 cup milk

Salt

1 teaspoon vanilla extract

Caramel Icing (recipe follows)

Place 1/2 cup plus 2 tablespoons of the sugar in a medium saucepan and let it melt over medium heat. Cook it until it is dark, being very careful not to let it burn. Add boiling water, stirring. Take care, as this will spatter. Stir until caramel is melted. Set aside to cool.

Preheat the oven to 350 degrees. Grease and lightly flour two 9-inch round layer pans.

Toss 1/2 cup of the flour with the pecans. Set aside. Sift the remaining dry ingredients together.

Cream the remaining sugar and butter until light and fluffy. Beat egg yolks lightly. Stir the caramel syrup into the yolks. Mix this well with the butter mixture. Add dry ingredients, alternating with the milk, beginning and ending with the dry. Fold in the dredged pecans and whatever flour may remain that you have tossed them in. Beat egg whites and salt until stiff, but not dry, and fold in. Fold in vanilla and pour into prepared pans. Bake until golden and cake tester comes out clean, about 25 minutes. Allow to cool slightly and remove from pans. Brush crumbs off layers.

Place one cake layer on a plate and pour half the icing onto it. Work quickly, allowing it to flow over the sides naturally. Use a spatula dipped in water to smooth the top. Place the second layer on and hold in place with toothpicks. Pour the remaining icing on top, allowing it to spill over the sides naturally. Remove toothpicks before serving.

Serves 12

Caramel Icing

2 cups dark brown sugar, tightly packed

1/2 cup granulated sugar

1 cup heavy cream

4 tablespoons unsalted butter

1 tablespoon vanilla extract

1 1/2 cups toasted pecans, coarsely chopped

Place the sugars, cream, and butter in a heavy saucepan and cook over low heat until butter is melted. Increase heat to medium and boil, stirring, until mixture reaches the soft ball stage (239 degrees on a candy thermometer). Cool for 10 or 15 minutes, then stir in the vanilla. Beat at high speed with an electric hand mixer until it is almost spreading consistency. Quickly stir in pecans. If it thickens too much, thin with a little cream.

Makes enough for two 9-inch layers

TOP LEFT: *Woodwork detail.* TOP RIGHT: *Preparing for lunch.* ABOVE: *Caramelized Sugar Cake.*

SOURCES

AIDELLS SAUSAGE CO.
1575 Minnesota Street
San Francisco, CA 94107
(415) 285-6660
Sausages of all kinds

AMERICAN SPOON FOODS
P.O. Box 566
Petoskey, MI 49770
(800) 222-5886
Dried fruits, cherries, jams, preserves,
and honeys

CHUKAR CHERRIES
321 Wine Country Road
Prosser, WA 99350-0510
(800) 624-9544
Dried cherries and other dried fruits

DURHAM MEAT CO.
160 Sunol Street
San Jose, CA 95126
(800) 273-8742;
in California (800) 233-8742
Buffalo meat

G.B. RATTO & COMPANY
821 Washington Street
Oakland, CA 94607
(800) 325-3483;
in California (800) 228-3515
International grocers

GOURMET MUSHROOMS
P.O. Box 391
Sebastopol, CA 95473
(707) 829-7301
Dried and fresh mushrooms of all kinds

THE GREAT SOUTHWEST
CUISINE CATALOG
206 Frontage Road
Rio Rancho, NM 87124
(800) 869-9218
Chipotle chilies, ground chilies, and all basic
Southwestern ingredients

TEXAS WILD GAME
COOPERATIVE
P.O. Box 530
Ingram, TX 78025
(800) 962-4263
Fresh venison, antelope, and wild boar;
smoked wild game

WILLIAMS-SONOMA
P.O. Box 7456
San Francisco, CA 94120
(800) 541-2233
Cookware, utensils, and food items

INDEX

OTHER BOOKS BY LEE BAILEY

"Lee Bailey understands the headlong
pace of modern life but never quite forgets the hunger
for what was best of our past."
Food & Wine